How to Thrive on Rejection

How to Thrive on Rejection

A Manual for Survival
by Alan Abel
Illustrated by Simon Bond
AUTHOR OF 101 USES FOR A DEAD CAT

DEMBNER BOOKS NEW YORK

Dembner Books
Published by Red Dembner Enterprises Corp., 1841 Broadway, New York, N.Y. 10023
Distributed by W. W. Norton & Company, Inc., 500 Fifth Avenue, New York, N.Y. 10110

Library of Congress Cataloging in Publication Data

Abel, Alan.
    How to thrive on rejection.

    1. Rejection (Psychology)—Anecdotes, facetiae,
satire, etc.   I. Title.
BF575.R35A24   1984   158   84-11320
ISBN 0-934878-44-7
ISBN 0-934878-45-5 (pbk.)

To booksellers everywhere
for their good business sense
in recommending this book
to appreciative customers

CONTENTS

Foreword

Alan Abel is a scamp, a rascal, a rogue. While he has supported himself at various times as a comedian, drummer, advertising copywriter, filmmaker, and free-lance publicity man, he is one of the great jesters of recent times, with an irrepressible flair for comic improvisation.

Abel's satirical spoofs, like any genuine works of art, need no other justification than their own existence.

Richard P. Frisbie
U.S. Catholic

Introduction

I've dealt with rejection all of my life. So have most people. But did you learn the knack of turning bad news into good? Probably not. That's why you need this book. If only *one* example provides inspiration, it's worth the price. Otherwise, ask for your money back.*

Most rejections center on sex, money, and employment. In between are a myriad of minor rebuffs, things like "no, you can't use the restroom, it's for employees only."

Your response should be: "I'm here to inspect the john; if you won't let me in I'll call the Department of Health."

Or, the bank is closed and it's exactly 3 P.M. A gruff guard won't let you in. (You forgot his Christmas present, remember?) However, if you carry two wrist watches, both three minutes slow, and stand on their validity, you'll win. I always do.

You have eleven items in the "10 only" express checkout line at the supermarket.

"Sorry," the clerk says. "You can't use this lane. Too many items."

"I'll pay for ten and return the eleventh," you reply.

The clerk will usually allow an extra item because there's no counter space for the sack of potatoes you're leaving behind.

"No, you can't enter the parade without a permit," says the uniformed officer.

Don't argue. Take your group and find a side street perpendicular to the parade. Then, when there is a space between marching units, jump right in!

"Stop," says the theatre usher outside. "The ticket line has ended. Come back for the next show."

You don't want to return in two hours. Offer an extra five

*You won't get a refund unless you write an acceptable 1,500-word essay citing your objections. Use bond paper, type double-spaced in triplicate, and allow six to eight weeks for appraisal by my mother. Neatness and spelling count. Include a stamped self-addressed envelope. Send to: Spencer Productions, Inc., 234 Fifth Avenue, New York, N.Y. 10001. Do not visit or phone if you value your life.

dollars to buy somebody's tickets waiting in front of you. There's always a frugal couple willing to sell anything for a profit.

"No, you can't pass out your circulars in this line of people."

Walk away, come back when the guard disappears. Hand a stack of circulars to the last person on line, ask him or her to take one and pass the rest on. Do the same at the front of the line. In a very few minutes everybody will have a flyer. If the guard chases you away, he won't stop the distribution of circulars among waiting patrons. They're legal; you're not!

"You can't have a table without a reservation."

"But I *have* a reservation, sir. It was phoned in yesterday by Rear Admiral Farnsworth, U.S. Navy, a very punctual person."

The maître d' can't find the reservation, obviously, and will locate a table. After all, any man who commands a battleship doesn't err over dinner reservations. But the restaurant staff could.

How to Thrive on Rejection is applied psychology, a course never taught in school. You've got the text without having to attend class or take exams. And your B.S. degree will be a major in *survival*. Just read and remember!

Alan Abel

April 1, 1984
New York, N.Y.

When You Have to Do Your Duty

I walked by the swanky Helmsley Palace Hotel in New York and asked the doorman for directions to the men's room.

"Sorry," he said, "it's for registered guests only."

"You mean, if I'm not registered, I can't go?" I asked with amazement and urgency.

"You can't go unless you're registered," he responded.

"My dog is registered. Could he do his duty inside?"

The doorman ignored this last comment and went about his job opening the door of an arriving limousine.

Several weeks later I returned to the entrance of the Helmsley Palace Hotel with my own private john, an old-fashioned outdoor privy mounted on wheels. Designed by conceptual artist Doug Quin, it was painted red, white, and blue. I had four confederates with me who passed out flyers that read:

HELP FREE TOILETS
There are no public lavatories on Fifth, Madison, or Park avenues. This is a disgrace to people and their bodily functions. Stores, restaurants, and hotels have locked us out of their johns unless we're customers. An American citizen should have the right to go anywhere nature calls, without behaving like a barbarian. Bring back civility now!

In a matter of minutes we were surrounded by the hotel's security forces. A crowd gathered to watch and several policemen arrived to maintain order. The security men ordered me to get out or they would dismantle my "Public People Pooper."

I stood fast, citing the U.S. Constitution: ". . . as a U.S. citizen I have the freedom to speak, see, hear, smell, touch, and do anything in public without restraint, and don't forget the Geneva Convention . . ." They weren't impressed. The city cops just shrugged their shoulders and fondled holstered guns.

A well-dressed assistant manager appeared and was apprised of the situation by his staff. The tension mounted as we continued to pass out flyers to the growing crowd of onlookers. One of the hotel's private guards approached me with his walkie-talkie in one hand, his other hand a menacing clenched fist:

"Get that goddamn pile of shit outta here!"

"Sorry. I fought in the war for the right to do my duty. And yours too if necessary."

"You're gonna die in another war—mine—right here on the sidewalk!" he screamed. "Now move it!"

"If that's the way I have to go, fine," I replied calmly.

"You've got one minute to go!" he shouted, looking at his watch and getting very red in the face.

"If I have to go inside the pooper it will take me at least five minutes—"

"Get the hell out of here, weirdo!" he bellowed at the top of his lungs as the crowd began shouting him down with taunts and jeers. Another hotel executive joined the growing melee and waved his underlings aside.

"How can we resolve this problem?" he asked pleasantly.

"Well," I said, "if we can use your men's room inside we'll move the Public People Pooper over to Park Avenue, where they have even fewer toilets. I think it is inexcusable for you to deny American citizens access to your restrooms unless they are registered guests. That's a totalitarian mentality. Today toilets, tomorrow the world. May I go in?"

"Fine, let's do that now," he said, forcing a weak front-desk smile while offering to lead the way inside the hotel.

At that moment a construction worker rushed up and pounded on the door of the pooper. He had to go badly. To circumvent this problem (the john was only a realistic replica), we had positioned a young lady opera singer inside. Any knocking on the door was her cue to begin singing "The Toreador Song" from *Carmen*. As she burst into song I explained to the worker that she had a long way to go. Fortunately, he couldn't wait and left hurriedly.

My associates moved our john down the block to Park Avenue followed by a stream of curious people, including several reporters. I had decided against visiting the Helmsley Palace men's room, although the manager assured us we were welcome back anytime, providing I left the outhouse at home.

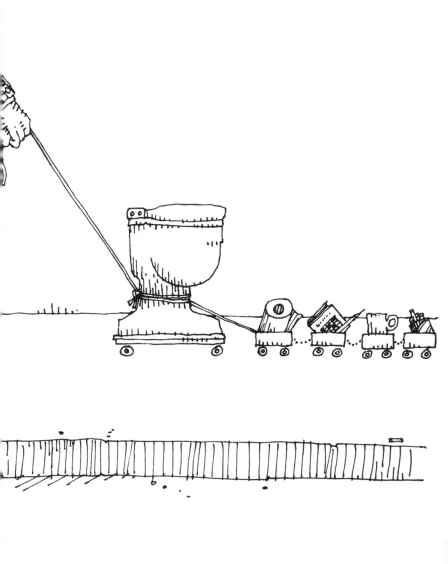

My Resurrection

Rejection is a nine-letter dirty word. It is an invisible germ that burrows its way into our subconscious and eats away at our capacity to perform and to realize our potential.

We are taught how to survive a fire, injuries, drowning, suffocation, and hydrogen bombs. But nobody prepares us for rejection. Once you've succumbed to insurmountable pressures, there's always therapy, enlisting in the armed forces, even suicide.

The last, unfortunately, penalizes your family and friends who continue living with layers of unexplained guilt. You are dead. Gone. No more pain or pleasure. And death is irreversible. You're not coming back.

I died and came back. On January 2, 1980, I remember opening *The New York Times* at a newsstand on the corner of Lexington Avenue and Fifty-seventh Street and finding my obituary. What a strange feeling to stand there in the snow, the white stuff falling all around, reading my own obituary:

Alan Abel, Satirist
Created Campaign
To Clothe Animals

Alan Abel, a writer, musician and film producer who specialized in satire and lampoons, died of a heart attack yesterday at Sundance, a ski resort near Orem, Utah, while investigating a location for a new film. He was 50 years old and lived in Manhattan and Westport, Conn.

Mr. Abel, a graduate of Ohio State University with majors in music and speech, made a point in his work of challenging the obvious and uttering the outrageous. He gained national recognition several years ago when he mounted a campaign for animal decency, demanding that horses and dogs, for example, be fitted with underwear.

At the time of his death, he was completing two books, "How to Thrive on Rejection" and "Don't Get Mad . . . Get Even!" Earlier volumes included "The Fallacy of Creative Thinking" and "Confessions of a Hoaxer." He wrote a humor column for The San Francisco Chronicle in 1966 and 1967 and was writing a similar column for the Gannett newspaper chain at his death.

With his wife, Jeanne, he produced and directed the film "Is There

Sex After Death?" They also produced a comic documentary on the Watergate affair, "The Faking of the President."

Before becoming a full-time satirist, Mr. Abel was an almost full-time musician, performing as a percussionist under the batons of, among others, Raymond Paige at Radio City Music Hall, David Rose and the leader of the Sauter-Finegan Orchestra.

In addition to his wife, he is survived by a daughter, Jennifer, a brother, Bruce, and a sister, Sally.

Quite frankly, I wanted to fulfill the ultimate fantasy, hovering overhead after departing, listening in to find out who really cared and what they had to say. I found out. And I was one hundred percent wrong!

One close family member responded to the news with, "So what else is new?"

People I knew all my life didn't bother to send a condolence card. Not even a few dead flowers. More than likely, I suspect, the feeling was, "there by the grace of God goes he, not me!"

On the other hand, there were comments like:

". . . he did more for humankind than the majority of Nobel Prize winners: he made us laugh. His spirit lives on . . ."

> Jay Sharbutt
> Associated Press

". . . one of my favorite alumni and certainly one of our most colorful . . ."

> Dan L. Heinlen, Director
> Ohio State University Alumni

A wealthy philanthropist who had often promised to invest in one of my projects, but never took the plunge, wrote: "My greatest regret is that I was never of more help. . . ." When I telephoned him with the good news he was outraged and hung up.

Casual friends whom I hardly knew sent some very moving letters to my widow. Maybe because they truly didn't know the guy well? No, I think they wrote from the heart. I've written to the family of a deceased person who touched me in some way, regretting I never knew him or her better. Perhaps you have done the same. I hope so.

My basic reason for this bizarre caper was triggered by a conversation I overheard in an elevator. Two lawyers were discussing on-going negotiations for the motion picture rights to my life, unaware of my presence.

"His counselor is holding out for too much money," said one lawyer.

"Let's cancel the deal, then," the other replied. "The story isn't dated; someday we'll buy the rights for peanuts from his estate."

As it turned out, the movie moguls revived negotiations the day after I died and then canceled again when I surfaced.

Setting up the obituary took several months of planning. The fateful day was to be January 1, 1980, when I knew key editors would be nursing hangovers from New Year's Eve. Second stringers on duty might not probe too deeply.

My wife, Jeanne, would have no part of this scheme; so she and daughter Jennifer, then seven, stayed away on an extended vacation.

A week before my demise, I established a secret hideway in a friend's New York apartment on Sutton Place South.

My grieving widow was played by a marvelous actress, Evelyn Jones, who appeared at newspaper and wire-service offices with a file of my press clippings. Her arrival was timed an hour after the news was telegraphed from Utah and an hour before press deadlines.

The "funeral parlor" was a mobile trailer parked near Donny and Marie Osmond's TV production studio in Orem, Utah. Fellow conspirator Gene Buck had installed a new telephone with the appropriate listing and answered all editors' verification calls solemnly.

Back in New York the All Souls Church on Lexington Avenue was booked for a wake and party afterwards. My will requested eulogies from actor friends Buck Henry, Cliff Robertson, and Jack Weston, ending with a grand party and a Dixieland band.

In actuality, the wake would have turned into a "roast" with the actors performing a Don Rickles–type tribute, leading to my resurrection. However, when the telegrams, flowers, and letters started coming in, I realized too many people were taking my passing quite seriously; going through with the wake would have been far too cruel.

Also, when I went to my bank for funds to pay the church,

caterer, and musicians in advance, the teller looked at me in amazement and said: "This account has been frozen! There must be some mistake."

Obviously banks read the obituaries too. She left to confer with a bank officer and I decided to leave. They would never accept or understand what I had in mind.

During the four days since I expired, there were over a hundred letters and mailgrams of tribute; a florist was holding several dozen floral arrangements with nobody willing to accept delivery. And Gene Buck called from his funeral home–trailer to advise he was surrounded by FBI agents, the Utah State Police, and plainclothes detectives. They wanted to question him.

Apparently, newsmen John Chancellor and Jack Anderson, both of whom knew me, had been checking over my obituary and wondering if this might be a hoax. Their suspicions were picked up by *New York Times* editor Sydney Schanberg and he sounded the alarm to authorities that I had been reported dead, but no body found.

It was time to bring down the curtain. I told Gene Buck to invite everybody in and tell the truth. It's one thing to fool the working press, but it's against the law to lie to federal authorities.

Telegrams went out to newspapers and wire services:

> REPORTS OF MY DEATH HAVE BEEN GROSSLY EXAGGERATED.
> THERE WILL BE A NEWS CONFERENCE TOMORROW 12 NOON
> AT THE BILTMORE HOTEL.

Buck called several hours later and said he had a nice chat with the officers. They were quite amused over the incident. One local sheriff stayed behind until the others had gone. He wanted one word explained that kept coming up in the conversations: "hoax."

The New York news conference was a standing-room-only affair. I fielded questions for an hour, explaining that the stunt was consistent with my past performances and not meant to embarrass *The New York Times* or any other news source. Spirits were high during this session and I returned to my office where a stack of calls requested additional interviews.

When the stories appeared in print and on the air, I was in for a lot of funereal backlash. Former friends wrote or called to suggest we remain just that. Others, such as television producer Maurice

Tunick, wired: "Great! Sensational! Terrific! Super! Outrageous! Keep 'em thinking!"

Life magazine publisher Chuck Whittingham wrote, "Delighted to hear you are still among the living after the proper amount of grief."

And Father Guido Sarducci said, "The last real resurrection was nearly two thousand years ago, and you didn't even have a cross!"

New York television host Bill Boggs devoted one of his programs to discussing the venture with me:

"I was very distressed when I first heard the news, Alan."

"I'm sure you were, Bill. Your letter to my widow was quite eloquent and I appreciate all the nice remarks. But your P.S. wasn't in the best of taste: 'What are you doing after the funeral?'"

Boggs and I have been friends for many years and he had suspected a gigantic put-on.

Joe Franklin, a perennial television personality in New York, edited a full-hour tribute consisting of various video clips of my appearances as his guest. Unaware of my news conference, he ran this program that very night. About halfway through, the television station was deluged with calls informing him I was alive. Suddenly, there was a direct cut to an old Hoot Gibson western film without any explanation.

A reporter from the New York *Daily News* called to verify my story. I assured him I was alive and asked what I could do for him. "Drop dead!" he replied grimly.

The Sun-Herald in Sydney, Australia, headlined its story: "A Hoaxer's Job Can Be Dead Funny" and *Die Süddeutsche Zeitung* in Munich began, "The late Alan Abel was dying to fool the New York Times . . ."

Jay Maeder, a reporter for *The Miami Herald*, wrote a Page One story on January 5, 1980, that set the tone for other articles around the planet:

REPORT OF DEATH . . . 'Fit to Print'

She walked into The New York Times' newsroom on New Year's Day, having somehow bypassed the security guards, a softly weeping woman bearing somber tidings: Alan Abel had passed away, she sniffed, and he was at peace now.

This would be Alan Abel, the celebrated practical joker: He who had tweaked America when he invented a nitwit organization called the Society for Indecency to Naked Animals and barnstormed the nation's talk-show circuit, earnestly urging citizens everywhere to clothe their pets. "Our only aim is to see that the naked animals of America are decently, simply and comfortably clothed," he said. People took him very seriously.

He who had run a wholly fictitious Bronx housewife named Yetta Bronstein for the U.S. Presidency ("Vote for Yetta And Things Will Get Betta!"). He who, at the height of the Watergate frenzy, had called a Washington press conference, gravely declared himself to be the Deep Throat of the Woodward-Bernstein reportage, announced that he was about to disclose very important things and then suddenly collapsed on the spot, leaving assembled newsgathers agape.

Alan Abel: Gone now to his reward, the weeping woman said, after a heart attack at a Utah ski resort. And only 50. A young man still.

The New York Times checked all this out, as it does with things. Yes, said all the relatives, he was a wonderful fellow. Yes, said the funeral parlor, we are handling the arrangements. Yes, said the church, a memorial service is scheduled.

"Apparently everybody was in on it," Times Editor Sydney Schanberg was saying Friday night. The Newspaper of Record professed to be largely undistressed by the hoodwink. "Our unofficial position is that our story was correct and that the gentleman at the press conference was an imposter," Schanberg said. "We're very sorry for the family."

However, *The New York Times* did publish a retraction of the obituary, restoring my right to life. As I mulled it over, I concluded that when I do go next time, for real, nobody will believe it. What better way is there to achieve immortality?

Winged Victory

A perfect example of rejection earmarked the early years of singer Mario Lanza's career. We were both members of Moss Hart's Army Air Force stage show, *Winged Victory*, and often roomed together, after I failed a Link Trainer pilot program by flying the simulated aircraft 200 feet underground.

Being the youngest member of the company at eighteen, I was in total awe of the stellar cast that included John Forsythe, Karl Malden, Edmond O'Brien, Lee J. Cobb, Kevin McCarthy, Barry Nelson, George "Superman" Reeves, and Irving "Swifty" Lazar.

In addition to playing on Broadway for six months, we toured the country for a year with all profits being turned over to Army Emergency Relief. A motion picture version of the show was filmed at 20th Century–Fox Studios, directed by George Cukor, with Lon McCallister, Jeanne Crain, and Judy Holliday playing featured roles.

Although Lanza sang in the choral ensemble, he never soloed because that assignment was handled by regulars Ray Middleton and Eugene Conley. Mario's voice was marvelous then and it was my first experience being so close to an eventual superstar.

We spent afternoons going to movies and Lanza sang songs with the audience, a popular feature in those wartime days. Time after time, people in the theater gradually stopped singing and allowed him to solo with the bouncing ball over words on the screen to "I've Been Working on the Railroad," "Sweet Adeline," and "Oh Dear What Can the Matter Be," followed by thunderous applause.

At the old Roxy Theatre in New York, his singing of "White Christmas" and "God Bless America" brought the packed house to its feet cheering. The lights went on and the manager asked Lanza to please sing all the songs alone. They rewound the film and he performed magnificently to another rousing reception.

One night, when singers Middleton and Conley were stricken with severe colds, Lanza got his big chance. He sang "O Holy Night" and "The Lord's Prayer" with such emotion the theater audience remained silent afterwards. Then, en masse, they roared their approval. Every single person was affected by his brilliance, and that strange silence was a sign of their mesmerization.

Subsequently, Lanza sang with a smaller variety unit that entertained at veterans' hospitals and army service clubs. The reactions were unanimously electrifying and it became difficult for the other variety acts to compete with him, in spite of talented performers such as Red Buttons, Peter Lind Hayes, the Slate brothers, Archie Robbins, and Louis Nye.

One Sunday afternoon, normally our day off, I was sitting in the General Motors Building office where *Winged Victory* was headquartered. I faced a silent typewriter trying to begin my writing career. Then I heard voices. They couldn't see me because of the cubicle arrangement. I remained quiet and listened:

"We've got to get rid of that bum. Lanza is bad news for all of our careers."

"Are the orders cut?"

"Yes. They'll come from Washington and he'll ship out as soon as we get to California."

"Remember, mum's the word. Walter Winchell or Westbrook Pegler would crucify us if there's a leak."

The group discussed other plans for trimming the company of undesirables, unaware of my presence. Sergeant Joe Bushkin made the final statement:

"And let's get rid of the kid, Abel."

"Why him?"

"He's a pain and I want him out."

I sat stunned. Me too? So this is show business! And these were familiar voices I admired on stage. How could they behave this way?

Lanza dismissed my apprehensions with a laugh.

"You've heard those audiences," he said. "They love me. Nobody is going to dare mess up my life now. They're just rotten with jealousy. Forget it."

Two months later in California Mario Lanza received his orders to ship out for overseas combat duty in an infantry regiment. It was a very sad day to see him go—dejected, dragging a barracks bag aboard an army truck. He was justifiably bitter, being sent off to the front lines, cut down at the start of a career by envious compatriots. And I felt quite miserable at not helping more after overhearing the plans to oust him.

A month later on the road, I found a note under my hotel door in Denver: "You're next, kid. Sgt. Bushkin plans to dump you in St. Louis or Kansas City."

It was signed "a friend." I managed to corner Moss Hart at breakfast in the Brown Palace Hotel dining room. He listened to me patiently as I went through the entire saga of events.

"Don't worry," Hart assured me. "Nothing is going to happen further. Remember, I met your mother in Boston and she warned me to watch over you."

Nevertheless I was concerned. Bushkin had successfully taken over the *Winged Victory* orchestra as conductor, leaving in his wake eminent composer David Rose and arranger Norman Leyden.

Opening night in Pittsburgh, concertmaster Elias Dann conducted the overture. Where was Bushkin? He had been shipped out to a Texas army base that morning with only two hours' notice.

The next time I saw Moss Hart was in Washington, D.C., during dinner at the Willard Hotel. He was sitting with writer Nat Hiken and press agent Bill Doll, also members of our company; I occupied a nearby table. When they got up to leave, Hart gave me a knowing wink and smile.

Hart had saved me, but I don't believe Mario Lanza ever overcame the shame and pain of being ostracized by his fellow performers in *Winged Victory*, despite his sensational success afterwards.

Jazz with Dignity

During the early forties, jazz was underground music relegated to dimly lit, sleazy night clubs. As a student at Ohio State University, following World War II, I initiated jazz concerts on stage that were widely imitated.

With fellow musicians Ziggy Coyle, Paul DeFrancis, and Bill Cole, I found the OSU Jazz Forum so that others could showcase their talents. Our weekly concerts were held in University Hall's auditorium and we were earning more money for the college's general fund than any other school activity involving music.

Jazz buff Fred Stecker, manager of the student union, gave us free meals in the cafeteria for an hour of dinner music—until the musicians' union called a halt. I appeared before a trial board to appeal:

"Gentlemen, you are against our playing music for food instead of money. How can you possibly overlook the economic trade agreements that exist between countries? No money changes hands. We musicians are trading our services for food equivalent to the monetary scale you have established. . . ."

Our pianist was also summoned to testify before the dour judges and he could only quiver: "I ate scale! I only eat scale!"

The board had to agree we were eating enough food to equal payment.

I tried to persuade name bandleaders to appear as guests during our jazz concerts without success. Their booking agencies turned down all requests for honorary visits and we didn't have the authority to pay out school funds.

Undaunted, I made contact with an Ohio State graduate who worked for Music Corporation of America in New York City, the largest band-booking agency. She regularly sent me the itineraries of name bands and I charted a date on their schedules when they were booked in Ohio. Then I sent a telegram directly to the bandleader:

> MR. JIMMY DORSEY
> MEADOWBROOK INN
> CEDARHURST, NEW JERSEY
>
> DEAR MR. DORSEY:
>   WE HAVE DESIGNATED SATURDAY MAY 11TH AS JIMMY DORSEY DAY ON THE CAMPUS OF OHIO STATE UNIVERSITY. SINCE YOU WILL BE AT MYERS LAKE PARK IN CANTON, OHIO, THE NIGHT BEFORE, COULD YOU HONOR US WITH YOUR PRESENCE THAT SATURDAY AFTERNOON?
>
>   SINCERELY YOURS,
>   ALAN ABEL, PRESIDENT
>   OSU JAZZ FORUM

This technique worked quite well. Most of the leaders brought their entire bands to perform: Gene Krupa, Jimmy Dorsey, Ray

Anthony, Stan Kenton, Elliott Lawrence, Norman Granz's Jazz at the Philharmonic, plus dozens of others.

During my senior year, twenty-five of our jazz musicians enjoyed a grand tour throughout the Northeast, concluding with a concert in Carnegie Hall. It was a fitting climax to our elevation of jazz from nightclub floors to the concert stage and the OSU Jazz Forum continues on campus today with a resident big band and a very loyal following.

The First Time

My first attempt to work as a standup comic out of college was frustrating. I had completed a successful engagement in the Adirondack Mountains at Scaroon Manor, a summer resort where *Marjorie Morningstar*, with Gene Kelly and Natalie Wood, was filmed. Producer David Benis encouraged me to try New York and contact him for assistance.

After moving to the Big Apple I called Benis many times over a year and he never returned my calls. Another producer, Manny Sacks with NBC Television, promised to arrange an interview and I waited several years for an appointment. He finally died.

The late Ernie Kovacs agreed to hear my routines over lunch at Jack Dempsey's Restaurant on Broadway. While Kovacs ate, conversed with his agent, and took phone calls at the table, I struggled hopelessly through monologues that were never heard.

Broadway producer Leonard Sillman offered to see my act if I could book a room and advise him accordingly. Naively, I rented a room at the Hotel Taft and called his secretary. She explained rather brusquely that "room" in show business meant a night club or theater showcase.

Angered by my own stupidity and not wishing to waste the hotel room, I went out looking for an attractive young lady. I found one shopping in Saks Fifth Avenue and she agreed to have dinner. Then we returned to my room.

During the fifties most hotels had house detectives and rules. A single room was meant to be just that. No unmarried couples or unregistered guests allowed.

At the stroke of midnight a loud knock interrupted our entrance into bed: "Mr. Abel, this is the house detective. You have someone in your room not registered. Open the door or I'm coming in with my passkey!"

My friend huddled under the covers while I made a dash for the shower. Panic stricken, my plan was to explain this person as my sister. The relationship would seem perfectly logical and platonic if I were bathing.

The open stall shower offered little refuge, for it had no curtain. I turned on the water and yelled, "Come on in."

The house detective bore a striking resemblance to Oliver Hardy of Laurel and Hardy fame as he stood inside the room laughing at me. Looking down I realized I'd forgotten to remove my T-shirt, shorts, and socks. He let us stay.

Running out of luck with auditions, I took to the road as percussionist with the Sauter-Finegan Band and a variety troupe that included singer Vaughn Monroe, impressionist Will Jordan, opera singer Helen Traubel, and comic Robert Q. Lewis.

During a one-night stand at Beloit College in Wisconsin, the headliners were stranded by a snowstorm in Chicago. An hour before the concert I was summoned by band manager Irv Dinkin to audition my comedy act immediately in front of Ed Sauter, Bill Finegan, and producer John Grogan. All three were in the field-house locker room sitting on toilets, suffering from a slight case of diarrhea.

The doors to their stalls had been removed by a crusading college professor to discourage homosexual encounters. Having auditioned and been rejected before, under miserable performing conditions, I figured I could endure one more indignity by doing my act for three guys during bowel movements. They humanely had me continue only a few minutes and then gave me their unanimous approval to start the show.

On stage, I was extremely nervous but several thousand students laughed in all the right places; it was a marvelous feeling to score for the first time with such a large and enthusiastic audience.

Producer Grogan doubled my salary and provided a featured spot on every show for the remainder of the six-month tour. This

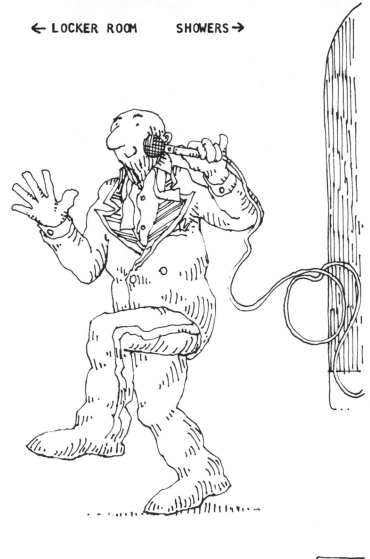

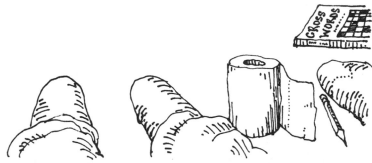

experience was vital to my continuing in New York. But it never really ended the process of having to audition for every new talent agent and producer.

New York . . . Love It or Leave It

Surviving as a performer, writer, or musician in New York City can be the pits. During the early fifties I lived in a single room near Columbia University with a community bath and kitchen that were areas of sheer bedlam. There was never enough hot water and Miss Schorr, an eighty-year-old spinster, would bathe for hours while loudly reciting bawdy limericks.

Every audition for a commercial or television show was a cattle call with an eternity of waiting, only to be dismissed by a curt, "Thank you. Next."

Vying with hundreds of fellow performers for only a few jobs, singers, dancers, actors, and comedians have to endure these rejections, praying to be accepted over others. It doesn't often happen and these slaves to their profession doggedly survive one day at a time, hoping the next will bring success.

A number of my friends had already bailed out of their chosen fields and left New York forever. I was still curious to see what tomorrow might bring, convinced if a person stayed in there long enough and worked hard enough, the odds would have to come up in his favor eventually.

A year later, down to my last two dollars, I sold a pint of blood for fifteen dollars. That was food money for a few days. It was a means to an end. Mine! I had learned to infiltrate company cafeterias for substantial lunches at low cost by wearing my three-piece suit, acting conservative, and speaking well of the company.

Emotionally too, I was bankrupt. Time to go home, back to Dad's general store in Ohio selling ready-to-wear merchandise. I was tired of living like a bum while trying to behave like a gentleman.

Normally I rode the subway uptown. It was faster than the bus and stopped right at my corner. This particular Friday I wanted a last glimpse of buildings and people; that meant taking the #104 bus up Broadway to 110th Street.

Much to my annoyance, a woman sitting next to me struck up a conversation.

"What do you do?" she asked.

"Oh anything, nothing, something. What difference does it make?" I replied a bit rudely, looking out the window.

"I'll bet you're an actor or writer trying your luck in this crazy city and not succeeding."

"You must have ESP," I replied facetiously, avoiding her gaze. I had had it with New York, there was no turning back, and a one-way bus ticket home was in my wallet.

"Look," she said. "I'm a talent booker and we could use you on a quiz show tomorrow night. It's a new television hour with Jan Murray hosting. We lost a contestant this afternoon—"

"Is there any money in it?" I interrupted.

"You get fifty dollars in cash when you show up—"

"I'll take it!"

Casting agent Rose Tobias gave me the information for the next day's rehearsal on a show called "Sing It Again" that was debuting over the CBS-TV network. It didn't interfere with my plans for beating the rent due on Monday and returning home, now with a few extra dollars.

I half-heartedly stumbled through the Saturday afternoon dry run. Two teams of contestants included a taxi driver, an accountant, and a housewife. Since I had degrees in speech and music, they labeled me a teacher.

After a break for dinner, we returned to the studio and the show went on the air, live, all across the country. We were each interviewed and then quizzed by Jan Murray on a variety of subjects until only the taxi driver and I remained.

"Now for the jackpot question," Murray said. "If either our teacher or taxi driver can untangle the mystery voice, we'll pay the winner five thousand dollars."

A recording was played with the voice speeded up to a high pitch. We had two minutes to decide.

"I think it's either Cecil B. De Mille or John Wayne," the cab driver whispered to me. "You take one, I'll take the other, and we'll split the prize."

I shook my head no. There was something about the rhythm of the garbled voice that rang a bell. I knew the sound but couldn't put a handle on the name. Arthur Godfrey? Dave Garroway? Lowell Thomas? No, none of those.

"Time's up!" said Murray. "Our taxi driver, Mr. Roth, has chosen John Wayne! Sir, do you mean the actor John Wayne, that great motion-picture star?"

"Yes, yes, yes!" shouted Roth. "That's the one!"

"Well, I'm sorry," said Murray. "That's not the one. Let's hear from Mr. Abel."

I quickly wrote down a name on the slip of paper. The pencil did the writing, not I.

"You say Edward R. Murrow? It's sort of scrawled here . . . is that your choice? I'll let you change it; we have time."

"No, that's my choice. Edward R. Murrow."

"Well, Mr. Abel, you have just won five thousand dollars!"

The band played, balloons went up, the audience cheered. I was in a state of shock and really can't remember what I said. But I know what I did afterwards. I walked over to the Greyhound Bus Terminal, found a ragtag couple with two kids sleeping on moth-eaten suitcases, and gave them my bus ticket.

The moral to this true story is that it's sometimes better to take the bus instead of the train. It could be the right one at the right time in your life. And don't be afraid to talk to strangers!

Two Dates for the Price of One

Tino was a swarthy, handsome, thirty-six-year-old used-car salesman with 225 pounds on a five-foot six-inch frame. His infectious smile, coupled with a winning line of gab, made him irresistible to most women.

I met him when we visited a singles bar on New York's East Side. While I struck out, Tino soon had two attractive young ladies in tow. He left early, an arm around each one, and gave me an encouraging look that said "keep trying."

The next day Tino called excitedly with some news:

"My boy, we got it made. Jane, the blonde, is hot for me, and I really sold Cynthia on you. Sorry you weren't included last night, but nothing happened. This weekend we go for the big score; you and Cynthia, Jane and me. It's all set."

Tino booked two double rooms at a small inn near Greenport, on the tip of Long Island. He would provide a car if I did the driving, and I could keep it for the rest of the week.

We picked the girls up after work. They were both secretaries with aspirations to model and either could qualify as a beauty contestant. Tino kept up a running dialogue of small talk and slightly off-color jokes to loosen things up during the three-hour trip.

Cynthia and Jane were pleasant enough but I suspected they were tiring of Tino's attempt to entertain. I couldn't think of much to say; it was his show and he seemed to have a way of romancing women. I didn't.

At the inn, following a candlelight dinner and polite conversation, Tino yawned, looked at his watch, and said, "It's midnight. Let's all hit the sack so we can get an early start on the beach. I'd like to jog for a few miles at sunrise."

We retrieved our bags from the car trunk and went up to our respective rooms. Tino and I had one, the girls the other. He went over to theirs for the planned switch and I could hear the conversation quite clearly:

"Tino, we're not that kind! You and Alan sleep over there. We are sleeping here. Now please get lost!"

He argued in vain. They threw him out. I was dejected. After all that driving and a heavy meal just before bedtime, I was going to end up in bed with my fat friend. A fine mess!

Tino came in and slammed the door. "Damned broads," he muttered. "I thought they knew what this was all about. Oh well, I'm tired. Let's get to bed."

Now imagine a 225-pounder in a small double bed with a sagging mattress. Tino immediately snored into a deep sleep with wheezing grunts and staccato gasps for air. Then he rolled over towards me, hogged most of the bed, and continued his obnoxious vocal barrage.

I got up, dressed, went down to the desk for another room. They were booked solid this summer weekend. Back upstairs I passed the two women's door and heard them talking quietly:

". . . he's so loud and boring, not like the first night we met. I'd sooner have sex with a whale. His friend is rather quiet and I wonder if he has a problem or something . . ."

Perhaps their rejection of Tino wouldn't be the same for me. A light bulb went on in my mind. It was worth a try and I knocked softly.

"Who's there?"

"It's me, Alan. Tino's fast asleep. May I please speak to you both for a minute? It's important."

Jane let me in. She wore a flimsy nightgown. Cynthia was under the sheet, apparently with nothing on. My heartbeat doubled.

"I want to apologize for Tino," I began. "He's always brash but inside is the tenderness of a Florence Nightingale. You see, he made this trip for me. I've been having a lot of problems with the opposite sex. It's mostly fear of rejection, inability to perform and just plain clumsiness when I do. Maybe I shouldn't unload this on you—"

"Oh please go ahead," interrupted Jane as Cynthia sat up in bed and partially exposed two very elegant breasts. I pretended not to notice.

"It's an awful dilemma to live with," I continued. "Tino was just trying to help me."

"You poor soul," said Cynthia, exposing a bit more breast. "We had no idea. . . . It just seemed like Tino was so pushy and obvious. We like to be seduced, not raped or taken for granted."

I sat on the bed and we all held hands as I launched into harrowing tales about ruthless women who abandoned me in bars and lovers' lanes, and threw me out of their apartments. Why? Because I was impotent most of the time and they wanted to score.

Cynthia and Jane had each undergone therapay and felt sorry for all I was going through. They were willing to experiment a little with the lights out, naturally.

Four exhausting hours later I staggered back to my room, completely cured. Daylight appeared and Tino was up getting dressed.

"Where the hell have you been?" he growled.

"Jane and Cynthia were lonely so I spent the night with them."

Tino laughed and threw me a friendly punch.

"That will be the day! They're probably gay anyhow. Look, we

give them the silent treatment and we're going back to the city right after breakfast. This place is for the birds."

Not a word was said during the long drive to New York. I dropped Tino off first and then the women. They insisted I come up for another round of therapy. It was a four-story walkup and I barely made it, in both senses of the word.

Be a Contestant, Be a Clown!

Becoming a contestant on a television quiz show involves a lot of hurdles. The obstacle course begins with interviews to determine your ability to laugh, smile, cry, jump up and down, clap like a seal, and emit ecstatic orgasmic screams when you win.

Interviewers are hard-nosed types who pretend to be friendly. Their real purpose is to determine if you can tolerate degradation.

Nice smiles win points. So do All-American looks. The right profession is important: no gamblers, porno film makers, unwed mothers, or—believe it or not—comedy writers. They're not considered fun types for family entertainment programs.

Contestants must sign all kinds of forms agreeing to pay taxes on any prizes received—and that, in some instances, can mean having to unload the prize. You take an oath not to promote any product of your own and agree not to be a contestant on other quiz shows.

This last condition is ridiculous. What about the celebrity regulars who dominate TV screens? Don't they ever wear out their welcome? You bet they do. If Richard Dawson or Zsa Zsa Gabor knocked on our door I wouldn't let them in the house!

Henry Morgan and Bob Barker would be welcome. Morgan is an endangered species who epitomizes a long-lost brand of sardonic humor; Barker is such a genuinely likable and capable performer he could run for U.S. President and win. They are welcome at our home anytime and can stay as long as they wish.*

I've worked with Henry Morgan on his weekly radio show out of New York and he is a delight. Bob Barker and I appeared

---

*Modified American Plan and plenty of hot water.

together on a short-lived CBS-TV pilot where I was placed in the audience and questioned by Barker:

"You, sir, what is your profession?"

"I'm an abnormal psychologist."

"Too bad. Are you recovering?"

"Not while Blue Cross pays."

"Why don't you come up on stage and we'll talk."

He grabbed my hand and I decided to stay put—something we hadn't rehearsed. Barker tugged unsuccessfully and the audience loved this byplay.

"Oh come on," he laughed. "Get up here."

"I get paid for my services," I ad-libbed, "and you want me up there for free!"

Over the years I've been on thirty or more quiz shows using a variety of names, disguises, and professions. It's the only way to reject the silly rules that forbid more than one appearance.

One of my first appearances was on "Who Do You Trust?" hosted by Johnny Carson and Ed McMahon back in the sixties. My wife and I pretended to be researchers seeking an answer to the growth of the Big Toe:

"When was the last time you looked at your Big Toe, Mr. Carson?"

"Well, quite a while, a few weeks . . ."

"Its horrible growth is due to negligence because you don't care and this indifference contributes to the delinquency of our toes."

"I care, I care!"

"If we don't relate to our toes they rebel by growing; we'll have mammoth feet in another twenty years and bring Darwin's theory full circle by swinging from the trees. People love high-rise apartments, women are wearing open-toed shoes . . ."

Carson and McMahon enjoyed the banter and we went on to win a stereo set, a week's vacation in the Bahamas, and five cases of peanut butter. We unloaded so much peanut butter on friends and neighbors they begged us to stop.

When Carson inherited the "Tonight" show he remembered my off-beat material and I was invited back several times, resulting in television commercials for Sylvania and Burlington Mills, the latter winning an Andy Award.

Aspiring actors, singers, dancers, and comics would do well to consider infiltrating the quiz-show circuit for television exposure. It's demeaning and dull but there are so few opportunities, why not make the most of what is available?

How to Win a Contest

The appliance store had broadcast a radio commercial offering a free 25-inch color TV set if you guessed two mystery melodies. I named "Yankee Doodle" as the first tune on a postcard to enter the contest.

A week later I got the call: "You've won the right to come on out and listen to our second mystery melody and win the TV set."

Driving from New York to Ronkonkoma, Long Island, isn't easy in a drenching rain. But I had to pursue this dumb quiz all the way.

The store turned out to be a former warehouse with piles of boxes and plenty of customers and guards. I joined a line of people waiting to win the television set. A man in a small glass booth had a recording on the turntable and nobody knew the tune. In about forty minutes it was my turn and I knew the music.

" 'Subconscious Lee' by Lee Konitz," I blurted out.

"Sorry," said the man gruffly. "Next!"

"Hey, wait a minute, I know I'm right."

"Get outta here, ya bum!" he shouted.

I left the booth quite angry. This fly-by-night outfit was hardly worth any more time and effort. While I stood around complaining I knew the tune, the manager and I had a brief confrontation.

"Sorry fellow," he said. "That's not the song."

"I can prove it," I retorted.

"Well, you prove it and you've got yourself a TV set," he answered.

They had scratched off the label so I had to find a copy quickly. "Subconscious Lee" was an extremely rare, collector's jazz recording.

Back to New York and an entire day telephoning record stores. One place in Greenwich Village had a copy, their only one left.

With the record hidden inside my briefcase I returned to

Ronkonkoma and took along a tape recorder camouflaged in a shoebox.

Another long wait. Same man in the booth, same record.

"Oh it's you again," he said. "Mr. Troublemaker with a capital T."

"Do you want to play my record?" I asked, taking it out. "It's the same as yours. Or should I play it for the district attorney?"

He shook his head negatively and signaled for the manager who came on the run. We now had quite a few witnesses in line who were extremely interested in this showdown.

My music matched theirs. They brought out the TV set, took a Polaroid photo with me alongside, and loaded the set into my car.

On the way back to New York the radio broadcast their contest announcement with another mystery melody, "America, the Beautiful." For half a second I was tempted to enter again.

Will the Real Alan Abel Please Stand Up?

I went out on the Chautauqua circuit some years ago lecturing on "the history of the snare drum and its effect on civilization today," a comedy routine in the style of Victor Borge. From schools to colleges to community organizations, it was three programs a day, six times a week, with Sunday reserved for complete exhaustion.

When I arrived inside the Hobart, Indiana, High School auditorium I was surprised to see a huge banner over the stage that said: "Welcome Home Alan Abel."

"How do you like it, Alan?" asked the principal.

"Fine," I said. "But this is the first time I've ever been to Hobart High School."

He laughed and slapped me on the shoulder, saying, "I always heard you had a good sense of humor."

Enter the custodian, a grisly man in overalls with a belt of tools.

"You're not Alan Abel!" he said with astonishment.

"No, I'm Winston Churchill," I replied. "Or maybe Harry S. Truman. Who are you?"

"I'm the engineer here," he said, looking me up and down. "I know Mr. Abel and you're not him."

"Well, I can show you my driver's license, credit cards . . . ."

"No, those things can be faked. Do you play the drums?" he asked.

"Yes," I said. And to prove the point I pulled a pair of drumsticks out that were part of my performance and played several rhythms on the lectern.

The principal suggested we go into his office. I couldn't imagine what sort of practical joke was being played. Educators are a serious group of people, especially during school hours.

Inside the principal's office he took a yearbook off the shelf. At the head of the graduating seniors ten years earlier was a photo of Alan Abel! I looked a little like him but it certainly wasn't my face. There were obviously two of us in this world, similar in age, height, weight, and percussion backgrounds. So, on with the show as planned.

Now I understood the strange event at Oklahoma University a month prior when this gorgeous lady came backstage and said she had been asked by mutual friends to meet and entertain me. I was baffled by her references to names I never knew—but it didn't spoil the evening.

May I take this opportunity to extend my belated appreciation to the other Alan Abel, wherever he is. And I still have the Welcome Home banner in the event my old high school in Coshocton, Ohio, ever decides to greet me someday.

Everybody Has a Price

Columbia, Missouri, is a three-college city, with the University of Missouri, Stephens College, and Christian College. I had lectured at the university and thought this was where I wanted to find a teaching position, settle down, marry, and raise a family.

The Missouri dean suggested a breakfast interview in his home at 7:30 A.M. I partied the night before until daybreak with friends who insisted I just take a cold shower, instead of napping, prior to my appointment.

Arriving promptly at the dean's home, we sat talking in the living room waiting for breakfast. I had just started to impress this

man who could change my status from itinerant lecturer to speech instructor, when an overseas telephone call interrupted us and he excused himself to talk privately upstairs.

Ten minutes went by, fifteen, and I dozed off. When I awakened with a start and glanced at my watch it was 10:30! I jumped up, terribly distressed. A note on the coffee table said, "Sorry. Didn't want to awaken you. We'll be in touch."

I tiptoed out the front door and never looked back. Nor have I ever forgotten this embarrassment. It was worse than getting caught in the shower wearing shorts and socks!

Goodbye University of Missouri. I wrote a letter of apology and also contacted the other two colleges. Stephens was well supplied with a long-term faculty. Christian never responded.

A few years later *Fortune* magazine ran a display ad by Christian College asking for substantial funds to bail them out of financial difficulties. They required one million dollars.

In a moment of frivolity and to test their moral fiber, I offered one million dollars in the name of Mrs. Yetta Bronstein, former independent candidate for president of the United States, providing they would change their name from Christian College to Jewish College.

A college official called my office in New York. Yes, they would accept the offer! He could be on the next plane east with the necessary papers. I quickly canceled the offer with this explanation: "Sorry. Mrs. Bronstein has decided to invest her money in pork bellies instead."

If the directors of a hallowed institution were willing to sell their tradition, perhaps my falling asleep at a dean's house couldn't be all that unforgivable.

Don't Leave Home without It

The late Maxwell Sackheim, an advertising and direct-mail genius, was a good friend, and during the early sixties he obtained an American Express card for me when I barely qualified.

While lecturing in Council Bluffs, Iowa, I dined at a restaurant that had just joined American Express. The manager was unwilling to accept a credit card because my home town,

Coshocton, Ohio, was stamped on it. He never heard of the place and abused me loudly before other customers at the cash register.

"I was an American-history major in college and I've traveled all through Ohio," he said bluntly. "You'll either have to pay cash or I'm going to call the sheriff. No checks either."

This being a weekend, I had very little cash and I was anxious to use the card. Something instinctively told me to just stay there and do nothing. A solution had to evolve.

At that moment the fates were kind. Copies of the Council Bluffs newspaper arrived on a stand next to the cash register. My attention was drawn to an Associated Press photo and story on the first page showing a Piper Cub airplane upended with law enforcement officials standing next to a man in handcuffs. The story read in part:

> . . . a flying bank robber held up a suburban branch in Hamilton, Ohio. He took off from a nearby field and flew approximately 135 miles before running out of fuel and crash landed near Coshocton, Ohio. Two bags of currency containing $25,000 were recovered. . . .

I signaled the manager and showed him the story. He blinked, shook his head in amazement, and accepted my credit card without comment.

"I find it hard to believe you majored in American history," I said in leaving. He didn't answer.

How to Save an Off-Broadway Disaster

Producing an off-Broadway show sounds easy enough. Find a good script, raise the money, audition and assemble a cast, contract a theater, rehearse, advertise, open the show.

My first revue in the late fifties, *Safari*, was a series of sketches and songs to introduce comedian Milt Kamen. A cast of twelve included singer Bobby Breen, a former Eddie Cantor protégé at the age of five, some twenty years earlier.

Backstage bickering began immediately and continued through opening night at the theater in New York's Barbizon-Plaza hotel.

Everybody gave one another a hard time and I was stymied as an inexperienced producer with lofty ambitions beyond my reach.

John Grogan, who later operated the Darien, Connecticut, Dinner Theatre, tried to help as did Leonard Levinson, a writer and producer friend. But things were totally out of hand.

Bobby Breen refused to sing a song written by Charles Strouse and Lee Adams, the talented composing team. Kamen was unhappy with sketches written by Hans Holzer (who subsequently became a ghost hunter). "They just aren't funny enough for my talents!" he screamed during rehearsals.

The cast was still at each other's throats when the curtain was about to go up on opening night before a sold-out house of five hundred. Breen decided he couldn't sing unless he was paid immediately, although all salaries had been deposited with the actors' union. Kamen wanted his money too, then Holzer and the others. The stage manager quit. I quickly wrote out checks and opened the curtain myself a half-hour late.

Clenched teeth, hissed dialogue, hysterical singing, and outrageous dancing gave the appearance of a barroom brawl on stage with the participants pretending to be satirical. The audience laughed *at* the show and critics had a field day with their devastating reviews.

I posted a closing notice even though we sold out the first week and had rented the theater for a month. By running ads with a reviewer's comments out of context—"Unbelievable performances!" . . . "Incredible gall!"—there was additional box-office business. But something dynamic had to be done, a gimmick to ignite ticket sales, because by the second night everybody in the cast settled down and gave excellent performances.

I remembered the publicity stunt engineered by master publicist Jim Moran for John Osborne's *Look Back in Anger*, when it seemed doomed to close on Broadway after mixed reviews. Moran secretly hired an actress to leap on stage and slap the leading man for his repulsive behavior. The show stopped, an astounded audience saw the young lady arrested, and this news went all over America.

Look Back in Anger ran for two and a half years, made John

Osborne famous, and earned Moran a hefty raise from producer David Merrick, who was never in on the scheme to save his show.

I called Jim Moran and we had lunch at Sardi's restaurant in the heart of New York's theater district. Moran is a huge man, six feet four, then weighing about two hundred and thirty pounds, with piercing blue eyes and a majestic beard. The last time I had visited him in his twelve-room high-rise apartment, he ushered me grandly into a sunken living room filled with antiques, life-sized statuary, and a gold-inlaid grand piano presented to him by Jordan's King Hussein.

The telephone rang at that first meeting and I couldn't help overhear Moran's side of the conversation:

"Yes, I have received the proper instructions by courier. The submarine will dock in Groton at twenty-four hundred hours. I shall be there."

That's only a slight glimpse of James Sterling Moran, a mysterious, legendary, and powerful giant in the field of publicity.

At Sardi's he talked nonstop for two hours and I didn't understand a word. Moran insisted on paying the check, we shook hands goodbye, and he dashed out the door with a parting remark, "Don't forget, my lad, sue the bastards!"

I walked over to the New York Bar Association building and asked the kindly, aged secretary if she could recommend a lawyer to sue the newspaper critics for attempting to close my show. Without batting an eyelash she went through a card file and pulled out a name.

"This man might handle your case if you can find him," she said. "We never can."

I called his number every ten minutes from my apartment. No answer. Occasionally the line was busy. I called again until the phone rang; still nobody picked up. Four hours later, after endless tries, a voice answered:

"Legal services, may I help you?"

"Where have you been?" I shouted in frustration. "I've been trying to reach you for hours!"

Sydney Rubin explained he had a very temporary office in a Grand Central Station telephone booth, having been evicted from his prior quarters, and he apologized for being in court all day. I was to meet him at 6 P.M. in front of the U.S. Post Office at Thirty-second Street and Seventh Avenue.

"It's quieter there," he said. "Too many people here. Bring a hundred fifty dollars in cash and I'll handle your case."

At the appointed hour I waited in vain for the sight of a legal type person. I approached several businessmen, asking each one, "Mr. Rubin the lawyer?" They weren't.

The only person left was a sad-looking chap in a tuxedo with a bass fiddle on a wheel. Could *that* be my lawyer? It was.

Rubin explained he would sue all the New York dailies for fifty thousand dollars each, charging conspiracy. The newspapers had twenty days to answer or lose by default. Their attorneys would take about ten days to file a general denial, then the judge would throw the case out of court for being frivolous and without merit.

He agreed that the mere filing of our papers should gain wide publicity as a first in the annals of show business. Rubin took down the necessary information, gave me a receipt for the money, and wheeled his bass across the street to the Statler Hotel where he was playing nightly.

In only forty-eight hours we had our news break, spearheaded by a United Press wire story. Curious theater patrons flocked to the box office in droves and I made arrangements to extend our theater run for another month.

Safari recouped most of the backers' investment. Max Liebman, producer of "Your Show of Shows" on television, attended a performance and hired Milt Kamen to understudy Sid Caesar. I received an offer to present *Safari* in Las Vegas, but without Kamen the deal fell through. Bobby Breen accepted a long-term contract to host a daily television variety show in Providence, Rhode Island. And lawyer–bass player Sydney Rubin sat in with our pit orchestra on closing night.

This experience proved that a show doomed by the critics can thrive in spite of them. Well, almost.

Critical Test for Critics

The rejection of any creative effort can be devastating to the artist, especially if he suspects the evaluator lacks talent and perception. Critics should meet certain standards; this test might be a start towards determining *their* composure under fire.

1. Circle your highest grade of education: 1 2 3 4 5 6 7 8 9 10

2. Did you take crib notes to class?____ Why?_____

3. (*Male*) Have you ever contributed to an unwanted pregnancy?____

4. (*Female*) Did you ever tell a lover you were "safe" when you knew you weren't?____ Why?_____
   (In 25 words or less, please)

5. (*Gays*) Are you remaining celibate during the great AIDS scare?____

6. So far how do you like this test?_____

7. Were you born in wedlock?____ Out of wedlock?____ Uncertain?____ Breast fed?____ Bottle fed?____ Uncertain?____

8. At what age were you first aware of the opposite sex?____ The same sex?____

9. Would you be willing to take a polygraph test at my expense if you pass?____ At your expense if you fail?____

10. Have you ever given a speech before an audience?____ Were you scared?____ Did you throw up?____ Before?____ During?____ Afterwards?____

11. Did the audience boo?____ Hiss?____ Laugh?____ Throw pennies?____ Attack you physically?____ Walk out in disgust?____

12. After rejecting someone's creation that became successful elsewhere, did you feel pleased?____ Dejected?____ Suicidal?____

13. Would you have any objection to my contacting your psychiatrist?____
    Name:_____ Telephone:_____

14. If you had to spend six months on a tiny deserted island in the South Pacific, which one of the following people would you choose as your companion?
    ____IRS examiner   ____Telephone operator
    ____Garbage collector   ____Dishwasher
    ____Customs inspector   ____Convicted felon

15. Recite one personal contribution to the creative world you are proud of:_____
    If none, write a three-hundred-word essay on one of the following topics:

    a. Why I resent other people getting ahead of me

    b. Why I sometimes feel like a motherless child

    c. Why I feel guilty taking money for my job

16. Have you ever refused a submission because postage was due?____

17. Have you ever used your company postage meter for personal mail?____

18. Have you taken paper clips, pencils, carbon paper, or stationery home?____

19. Do you make personal phone calls from the office?____

20. Did you ever consider reimbursing the company for answering "yes" to #17, 18, or 19?____Yes. ____No. ____Maybe. ____None of your business.

21. How guilty do you feel now?_____

22. Problem: You have had a very frustrating day and desperately need to vent your spleen. Choose one action below that would relieve the tension:

    ____Cry

    ____Scream

    ____Kick the water cooler

    ____Make an obscene phone call

    ____Resign

    ____Join the Moonies

23. (*Female*) How much would you charge to pose for a *Playboy* centerfold?____$50. ____$100. ____$150. ____$200. ____$250.

24. (*Male*) How much would you charge to pose for a *Playgirl* centerfold?____$250. ____$2,500. ____$25,000. ____$250,000. ____$2,500,000.

25. If you had your life to live over again, why wouldn't you?
        (Please limit to 10,000 words)

Don't Tread on My Manuscript!

SINA, or the Society for Indecency to Naked Animals, was an imaginary campaign to clothe all naked animals for the sake of decency. Nobody exposed this tongue-in-cheek organization for several years until I appeared on "Kup's Show" in Chicago with Art Buchwald and let the cat out of the bag.

Buchwald encouraged me to write a book, suggesting the title, *The Great American Hoax*, and a few weeks later his nationally syndicated column revealed the clothed animal crusade:

THE GREAT AMERICAN HOAX*

In 1964 a young American writer named Alan Abel formed a society called SINA, the Society for Indecency to Naked Animals. Mr. Abel proclaimed that his organization was for clothing all animals in public for the sake of decency and that it would militantly pursue its goals.

For the next four years Mr. Abel's campaign, abetted by himself, his wife, and the doorman of his apartment building, caught on like wildfire.

The nation's communications forces, press, radio and television, gave it wide publicity, and many people took the campaign seriously and offered money and support. Others suspected a publicity stunt which would soon reveal a commercial link-up, and still others felt that Mr. Abel was some kind of nut.

But despite skepticism, Mr. Abel managed to exert great influence on different organizations. He had an unclothed papier-maché horse removed from a Fifth Avenue window in New York when he threatened to picket the store. Zoo directors became furious when he said that taking your children to the zoo was like taking them to a burlesque show. Clothing manufacturers offered to tie up with SINA if they would give their endorsement. The Post Office banned SINA's magazine showing a clothed horse on the cover. A lady in Santa Barbara wanted to give SINA $40,000 for the cause. And so it went. But through it all everyone kept wondering what Mr. Abel's angle was.

Mr. Abel told us in Chicago that his organization was formed to show how gullible the American people really are.

*Reprinted with permission from Art Buchwald.

"You could call it a great morality play," he said. "I was trying to satirize our customs. People say one thing and do another. We find this in politics, business, sex, and in every part of our life. Even the title of my organization was a contradition. It means the opposite of what I was trying to do. And although people laughed at us, they never understood us. The naive believed we were for real, the smart alecks were sure we had an angle. Hardly anyone guessed we were pulling their leg."

Mr. Abel said the gag didn't cost him much money. "It may have cost about twenty dollars a week, and since neither my wife nor I drinks, that wasn't much. We returned all money sent to us and turned down all commercial tie-ups. But even I didn't realize how big this thing could become. I discovered that any crackpot group, so long as it sounded official, could put pressure on any important organization in the United States and scare the hell out of them.

"I discovered that people not only didn't read, they couldn't hear. On Labor Day I got a SINA band together and marched in a Labor Day parade in New York City. I had a cello in the band, a bugle, two trumpets and a snare drum, and we played 'The Stars and Stripes Forever,' each in a different key. But because we were carrying the American flag, everyone along the way applauded."

When Mr. Abel wanted pickets, he hired them at $2.25 an hour. His "president," Buck Henry, was an actor who played the role on TV shows, interviews and press conferences.

"People can't understand why I did it. When I tell them that all I was doing was satirizing the gullibility of the American people, they won't believe me."

We asked Mr. Abel if he considered his hoax a success.

"No. I consider it a failure—a very successful failure, but still a failure."

"What have you proved?"

"I think I've proved that one person with a wife and a doorman can turn the country upside down. I've also proved that America gives in to nuts very easily and is afraid of them.

"The question is how do you awaken people when they can be taken in so easily? I don't think, even though the secret is out, that people will change their attitude toward SINA. Once you plant the idea in people's minds that animals should be clothed, it's hard to turn back."

It took six months to finish my first full-length manuscript recounting the zany adventures with SINA. Lacking an agent, I submitted it directly to major publishers, starting with the A's.

After thirty-four rejections I was ready to toss the project into a trunk for my heirs. But there were two publishers left; Simon and Schuster, and Viking Press.

During the two-year period, three copies of the manuscript had made the rounds; I sent the original to Simon and Schuster as the other copies were quite worn.

Six weeks later I received a call from the publisher and a pleasant female voice said they were still considering my book. Another four weeks passed and the same voice called to advise they were getting close to a decision. "We need more time," she added.

I wanted to shout, "Take all the time you want! Just publish my first book!"

But I deferred to a casual, "Please keep me informed."

Three weeks later I couldn't stand the silence any longer. I called. The friendly voice was no longer with the company. A brisker type put me on hold and went to the files. My manuscript was in editorial; would I give them two more weeks, maybe three?

"Of course," I said pleasantly, hoping to hide my anxiety.

After four weeks I received the manuscript back with a form letter turning it down. A number of the pages were dog-eared; a huge coffee stain had filtered through the first twenty pages; several of the photos were cracked; and someone had balanced their bank statement on the back page.

My manuscript being treated as scrap paper and a coffee mat! It was time to fire a well-aimed broadside:

Mr. Leon Shimkin, Chairman of the Board
Simon and Schuster
1230 Avenue of the Americas
New York, New York 10020

Dear Mr. Shimkin:

By way of introduction I am an unpublished writer with a bone to pick. Your editors kept my manuscript, *The Great American Hoax,* for four months before rejecting it. I can live with that but I resent the shoddy way in which my creative work was treated.

There were coffee stains, torn pages, bent photos and personal banking performed on my original copy that I had personally typed and submitted in good faith it would be respected.

Is this any way to run a publishing company? Absolutely not! It seems to me that since you started business in 1924 and have done well without any contributions from me, you may well continue without needing my services. And I too shall survive without requiring that you publish my books.

Yours very truly,
Alan Abel

My wife advised against sending the letter. She felt it would be counterproductive towards ever being published. We agreed I would sit on the letter for twenty-four hours. The next day I mailed it.

Three days later I received a call from Shimkin's secretary:

"Mr. Shimkin would like you to have lunch with his executive vice-president, Mr. Harold Roth."

"Where?" I asked. "In Central Park at dawn? And what are the weapons?"

"No," she laughed. "At the Down Under Restaurant in Rockefeller Center, tomorrow at one P.M."

I attended the luncheon expecting to exchange some bitter barbs. On the contrary, Harold Roth was pleasant and apologetic. They were now willing to publish my book! I sat stunned as Roth offered a ten-thousand-dollar advance and a grand promotion tour.

He waited for an answer as I was trying to summon a voice that wouldn't crack or turn soprano.

"Mr. Roth, you've got a deal. Would you mind if we went to your office and signed a contract because my wife is never going to believe this turn of events."

When I returned to our New York apartment with a check and signed contract in my pocket, I had to play a little with Jeanne.

"Well, dear," she said, "I can see from your expression you had a rough time. What happened?"

"It was incredible," I answered with feigned pain. "The unmitigated gall of those people at Simon and Schuster to treat me like a yo-yo."

"I don't understand. What happened?"

"Well, you know how they rejected the book. *Now they want it!*"

"You mean they want to publish?" she shouted. "I don't believe it!"

"Well you better believe this!" I answered with a war whoop and took out the check and contract.

We celebrated by paying a pile of bills and vacationing at the Trapp Family Lodge in Stowe, Vermont, where I made some final corrections on the manuscript.

The Great American Hoax was published in hard cover and optioned for a movie by Paramount Pictures. Although the film was never made, I had the satisfaction of proving that it is possible to thrive on rejection.

Smile! You're Not on "Candid Camera"!

For years the *National Enquirer* wanted to fool Allen Funt, of "Candid Camera" fame. But the master spoofer was too wary of anybody tricking him.

Enquirer editor Maury Breecher offered me the challenge with a substantial bonus for success. At first I considered delivering a concert grand piano to Funt's house and filming a surprised look on his face when he opened the door. However, the logistics of handling such a huge instrument and the chances of his not being home were too risky.

Another thought was sending a talking llama to his office with a ventriloquist animal-handler or a tap-dancing robot with a midget inside. Funt's office schedule was too erratic for either of these stunts. Any failure on my part would have put him on instant guard against another attempt.

My final plan was simple and safe. Attractive free-lance reporter Paulette Cooper would interview Allen Funt for a magazine story.

One of their dinner meetings was at the posh Park Lane Hotel on Central Park South in New York City. I arranged with the maître d' for a huge birthday cake, a strolling string ensemble, and all waiters to converge on Funt's table when I gave the signal.

As Paulette Cooper engaged Mr. Candid Camera in conversation, we made our move and everybody sang "Happy Birthday," including other diners. Funt looked up in astonishment and said, "But it's *not* my birthday!"

At that moment he was photographed by two *National Enquirer* cameramen from the far side of the dining room using a telephoto lens. They captured a perfect picture of Funt, mouth wide open, eyes bulging in a shocked facial expression.

When I explained everything to Funt he was graciously amused that this was truly a first in his life. And we all enjoyed the birthday cake plus an evening of anecdotes that television censors would never approve.

The *National Enquirer* published the story and photograph on its front page with a gleeful headline: "Funt Fooled by Funster!"

At times, people have played practical jokes on me. After Art Buchwald revealed my comic campaign to clothe naked animals, I received an invitation to appear on a BBC-TV interview program in London because the British press had taken that crusade quite seriously.

When I arrived at Shepherd's Bush Studio an hour before the scheduled taping, an attractive young lady showed me to a client's booth where she poured two drinks and held my hand seductively. One sip of the Scotch and I almost fell over from its super strength. The long-haired blonde beauty insisted I "drink up," but I just pretended to swallow.

It was time to tape. My interviewer, a kindly old gentleman in his late seventies, sat waiting in one of two director's chairs that faced each other. Before we could be introduced, a voice came over the public address system, "Quiet now, tape rolling, ten, nine, eight, seven . . ."

"Mr. Abel, I understand that your campaign to clothe all animals was interwith on the decided and shocked insense. Is that true?"

As I had just returned from Scotland where I couldn't understand their brogue, I assumed this man was a Scot or maybe senile. Unlike television in the States, the British held on to their personalities until they died. It was not uncommon to see octogenarians reading the nightly news.

Rather than embarrass him, I answered as though I understood the question:

"You could say that, sir. Furthermore, a nude horse is a rude horse and some of our most influential supporters are English."

"Well," he continued soberly, "that may be true, but I ask you if SINA with all its conversomes could manage to suffern without conceiving."

It suddenly dawned on me. The BBC was playing a practical joke and I faced a master double-talk artist! There was only one way to cope; answer every question intelligently, no matter what he asked.

Back and forth we went, he with some of the finest double-talk ever heard on the British tube. Only much later that evening did I learn he was one of England's best, Sir Stanley Unwin, featured in a long-running television series, "Carry On."

"But Mr. Abel, you have been quoted in the States as saying that animals have no sense of sin, that the whole world is their bedroom. Now would you consider this ansin on morals a resolution?"

"No," I answered. "We as humans go around censoring statues by putting fig leaves on them out of a sense of personal guilt over our own sexual embarrassment."

From time to time, out of the corner of my eye, I could detect the cameramen holding their sides, desperately trying not to laugh out loud.

Unwin concluded the half-hour interview with his only straight question:

"Are you convinced that television interviewers are so incredibly gullible?"

"I think they are a little too smug at times, perhaps brainwashed by their invincibility. For example, my latest campaign concerns the growth of the big toe, leaping forth at the horrendous rate of a hundredth of an inch a year! Did you know that?"

"No, I didn't," stammered Unwin, suddenly trapped into being interviewed.

"Well, you should be concerned," I admonished him, "and stop the growth by identifying with your big toes; let them know you care, allow them to perform simple tasks around the house like scratching your spouse's back, turning the telly on, and cracking peanut shells."

"Yes, I'll do a deep jerring on it," he promised. "And thank you very much, Mr. Abel, for underlining the human behind."

Later that evening the interview was aired with announcer Charles Michaelmore making introductory remarks that I hadn't been aware of:

"I wonder if Mr. Abel still believes we're all such a gullible lot as he watches from his hotel room. After we recorded this interview, Mr. Abel gave no sign at all that there was anything odd about the questions. He left our studios happily talking about his voyage back to America tomorrow on the *Queen Elizabeth*."

My wife and I hoped for a quiet five-day trip home aboard that lovely ship. No such luck. Many of the passengers had witnessed the sparring match with Unwin and said it topped anything ever seen for sheer comic insanity.

The only retaliation on my part was a whispered rumor in the ship's dining room that the *Queen Elizabeth* was being tracked by an Egyptian submarine flying a white sheet on its periscope. (The Arab-Israeli war was then in progress.) Passengers with binoculars were soon peering out over the waters trying vainly to sight the sub.

Eventually the captain had to post notices on bulletin boards that no conventional submarine—even if Egypt had one—could match his ship's top speed. As proof he cited her World War II record for transporting troops to Europe without a convoy.

Unemployment Insurance Intimidation

Applying for unemployment compensation can be an embarrassing experience. From the office manager on down through the clerks, they malign and harangue the jobless. Observing endless lines of rejected, anxious, unemployed people waiting at windows to sign for checks is a pitiful sight. If you've had to apply for unemployment compensation, you know you can spend hours abused by an ingrate beneath your skills and intelligence, only to learn you've been in the wrong line!

One young lady friend, an actress, returned to New York after a year touring with a Broadway musical. The company disbanded and she was eligible for unemployment insurance. After waiting in line (the wrong one) for two hours, she spent another three in the right one, was told to be seated for an interview, then advised to come back the next day because it was time to close the office!

Another three hours the following morning—she missed two critical auditions and possible jobs—the office closed for lunch and finally at 3 P.M. she was interviewed:

CLERK: I see you've worked in Chicago, Los Angeles, San Francisco, Detroit, and ten other cities. How long did each job last?

ACTRESS: Well, we would play the show for two weeks, sometimes three or four in each city.

CLERK: (*Loudly*) You mean to tell me you could only hold your job for a few weeks in any one city? You're not very reliable are you? You're gonna sit down for more interviews and take a test to see what kind of job you can do where you don't go running off every two weeks.

My actress friend was reduced to tears by this incredible stupidity and she never returned, fortunately landing another Broadway show a month later.

State employment offices are supposed to help people find jobs. And they will if you don't mind driving a tow truck, running an elevator, or clipping poodles. If you refuse reasonable offers, they can deny your benefits.

Having been eligible for unemployment insurance, I received the red-carpet treatment after complaining to the then governor of New York, Hugh Carey:

Dear Gov.,

Hi old buddy. Are you getting much these days? I mean with all your duties, pressures, etc. I certainly hope so!

Now that wasn't very respectful of me, was it, sir? Well, I apologize; but I did so to make a point. Let me ask how you could allow the people who administer unemployment insurance to behave like crude animals? They are uncouth, belligerent, inhumane, incompetent, and a detriment to your administration.

The people in those lines are not out of a job because they want to be. And unemployment compensation is an insurance fund created by our lawmakers to tide jobless people over until they again find gainful employment.

If you care, and I know you do, you'll clean house from top to bottom. With unemployment at an all-time high, there are literally thousands of deserving, educated, and compassionate people who could function loyally inside unemployment offices.

Why not turn the present crop of featherbedders out to pasture and give unemployment insurance a healthier image?

To prove my case, I have a tape recording of unhappy jobless claimants being berated by your employees. Would you like to hear these tapes?

Respectfully yours,
Alan Abel

cc N.Y. State Employment Office

One of Governor Carey's aides called me to request the tapes. Unfortunately, like Nixon's eighteen and a half minutes, they had been accidently erased.

However, my next few months found shorter unemployment lines and much more courteous clerks. They seemed particularly friendly to me.

One anecdote worth relating applies to a jobless person who has been fired and denied benefits.

I had toured with Sammy Kaye's orchestra performing a comedy routine along with Sid and Marty Krofft's puppet show. The three of us were outshining Kaye's role as bandleader and he proceeded to put us down in front of audiences.

At the Roosevelt Hotel's swanky Blue Room in New Orleans, Kaye gave me a string of negative comments before a sold-out dinner show: ". . . and this fellow Abel, he plays the drums too. Not very well, does a lot of faking—"

I had taken the slurs long enough. I took the microphone away from Kaye and said to the audience: "Wait a minute, ladies and gentlemen. *I'm* not the faker. Sammy Kaye is!"

Then I grabbed his expensive hair piece and dangled it in the spotlight as the crowd became hysterical with laughter, thinking it was part of the show. Kaye, completely bald, ran to his dressing room muttering obscenities.

I was fired and denied unemployment insurance, "having been relieved of duties for incompetence." On appeal, I demonstrated my deed with a borrowed hair piece—using the bald head of a board member representing the unemployment commission. Supported by the Krofft brothers, along with affidavits from the band members that I had not been incompetent, I won a reversal decision.

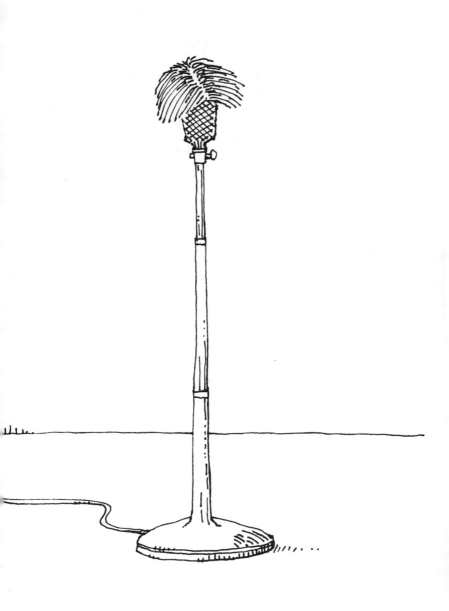

Party Poopers

Remember when the teacher went out of the room and told everyone to study? Instead, it was party time and the rafters rocked with hilarity. A lookout warned "here comes teacher" and total silence reigned with all heads buried in books.

But there was always one rat who told. Teacher's pet spilled the beans and everyone was given an extra assignment as punishment. Goody Two Shoes got the usual "A" and went on into life as a perennial party pooper.

There continues to be a spoilsport throughout life—in community organizations, social clubs, the office, you name it; he or she is determined to play rotten egg.

I had one at the University of Miami during a recent lecture. Things were going well with the audience as I took aim at a variety of subjects:

". . . fat people should be deported because they exhale too much CO_2 and cause air pollution along with automobile exhausts . . .

". . . certainly the Aborigines are still backward, although the men have learned to tie a string at the base of the penis to remember something; they remember it's very painful . . .

". . . we need sex education in schools, beginning with the elementary grades. Why not publish the facts of life in a graphic cartoon booklet entitled "Show Me Yours and I'll Show You Mine" with a pop-up feature . . .

". . . that Korean airliner shot down by the Russians was a terrible tragedy; but should we go to war and destroy the world? No. I think all nations could now take turns shooting down rival airliners once a month as a blood-letting exercise to avoid total annihilation. First we knock out a Russian passenger plane in retaliation, then draw lots for the next one. It could be KLM, Air India, British Airways, Qantas, and so on. Better to lose 268 people a month that 268 million and the world!"

My audience responded in good spirits until the question-and-answer period. An instructor stood up from the center of the crowd to challenge the stage:

"Mr. Abel, you've made fun of politics, religion, advertising, and education. Is there nothing sacred with you?"

I could hear the collective gasp, then silent surprise and disappointment from the students. It was apparent to all we had a rotten apple present who single-handedly stopped the show—and the fun.

"Sir," I replied, after a pause for feigned meditation, "I have respect for many things in life. And to prove your allegation is without foundation, you'll notice I haven't made fun of Spics, Wops, or Polacks."

The crowd's roar of laughter and applause punctuated my reply to establish their approval and our party pooper stormed out.

Another time, at the Pittsburgh Playhouse, I was addressing a convention of radio and television executives. After a rollicking half-hour of humor, I received this question from the back of the house:

"We here in Pittsburgh have gotten along perfectly well without far-out ideas such as yours. I would like to know if you can document any of your success stories with facts, names . . ."

On and on he droned for five minutes before uttering the final words, "And what do you have to say to *that*?"

From the ominous silence of the overflow audience, I sensed their embarrassment.

"I'm sorry, sir," I replied. "I wasn't listening."

The crowd shared my disdain for the questioner by cheering and applauding loudly.

Although this was a frivolous occasion, intended to amuse, not anger, the lesson to be learned applies as well to matters more serious.

If we allow a minority faction to interfere, disrupt, and perhaps destroy a meeting of the minds, then we're not far away from the repression of our basic freedoms that can lead to anarchy.

In such situations, I've often used the mental picture of myself as a matador. The bull is coming at me, snorting, his sharp horns within inches; but I trick the beast, leaving him to charge past, inflicting no harm.

How to Avoid Being Dunned

All of us have or will face a financial crisis in our lives when there is no escape. Loss of job, savings, and self-esteem place one in the pits. Especially if you're over forty, have established a home, family, and kids, and require a regular cash flow for survival.

Banks won't make loans to the unemployed. Friends and relatives resist more-than-temporary handouts, even though you're going to face skid row without immediate financial relief.

Of course there's always panhandling. As a social satire on unemployment, I wrote *The Panhandler's Handbook*, under the pseudonym Omar the Beggar, offering professional expertise on how to beg. I've since been amazed to observe street people using the ploys recommended in Omar's book.

After you've been rejected for loans or jobs and you're at your wits' end to stave off creditors, sit down and compose a form letter as follows:

To My Creditors:

I am presently facing a very critical financial vacuum. This situation is temporary and I need your support in order to overcome my dilemma and resume a compatible financial relationship with you.

Basically, I require a six-month moratorium on all of my accounts payable. This time period will permit me to reorganize my life, gain a new foothold on obtaining a cash flow, and prepare to fulfill all outstanding obligations.

I have considered going into Chapter 11, but this is a defeatist's approach and unfair to you as well. I want to pay every penny owed, not just a portion. But I need some time and relief from any pressure to pay now.

If you can accept the courage of my convictions I will be grateful. More important, after I regain my financial control, your kindness will be rewarded with interest and principal in full.

Respectfully yours,

I've had to use this letter twice in my life. It worked both times. Creditors would prefer to avoid bankruptcy court and the legal fees they would incur, because their share of the pot would be minuscule. They can commiserate with your suffering and offer a helping hand. There is still compassion available if you apply for it.

The Check Is in the Mail

Public utility companies are sticklers for the amount paid and date check was mailed. Otherwise your service gets the guillotine after an allowance of seven days for post-office delivery. The pony express was faster and surer. Even carrier pigeons could guarantee quicker service.

However, the deterioration of postal services is a blessing in disguise for the impoverished consumer who can mail checks late and predate them to verify that "my bill was paid on time."

This process provides busywork for employees tracking down your payment, affords you more interest on money in liquid accounts, and allows extra time to cover the checks issued.

Everybody has experienced the dilemma of an overdue telephone bill:

"We have not received payment and your service will be terminated tomorrow."

"That's impossible. I mailed the check two days ago at the corner mailbox."

"I'll allow you one week more to receive this check, otherwise you can kiss your dial tone goodbye."

"You are a very understanding person and I intend to recommend you for a promotion."

A week later your check hasn't arrived and Ms. Venom comes on the line again:

"I warned you. Your check wasn't in the mail today so we will have to cut off your service at noon unless payment is delivered to our office in cash, or by certified check or money order. If your service is terminated there will be an additional charge for restoration plus another deposit to insure next month's payment."

There's no compassion in Ma Bell. Reach out and touch someone? You'd like to reach out and punch someone! But don't despair, there is a survival technique. All you need is a tape recording of a crying baby. Have this tape playing in the background as Big Sister nails you to the proverbial cross:

"Do you hear that baby crying? Well, I intend to hold you personally responsible if you shut anything off and that child suffers further and we have to call a doctor. Now I want your name and badge number just in case we have to sue."

During my leaner years this ploy kept the lights burning for months after a cutoff notice, and my telephone operating for over a year before I could pay all the past-due bills.

It's really a shame you can't be totally honest:

"Look, I don't have the money now, I'm looking for a job, funds are due from home, I expect a loan, just let me live another few weeks without hassles and I'll pay."

Forget it. Public utilities are unconscionable and their employees' brains are exchanged for computer tapes. Consider this conversation I recently had with a Con Edison official:

"So how do you like your job down at the hydroelectric plant?"

"I'm sorry, sir, I cannot discuss my work during business hours."

"Any spills or leaks you can pass along since the conversion to nuclear power?"

"If you have nothing further that relates to your business, I will have to terminate this call."

"It sounds like you've been programmed. Or is this a recording?"

"Thank you for calling and goodbye."

Public utilities will bend over backwards to accommodate crying youngsters when you can't pay the bills on time. But they don't give a hoot for anyone old enough to vote.

Barefooted Tom Snyder

The Philadelphia Advertising Club asked me to write and present a satirical spoof on advertising during an annual awards banquet.

For this occasion, newsman Tom Snyder was to give the introduction. We sat together at the speaker's table conversing, when I suddenly developed a nose bleed. It wouldn't stop. Coffee and dessert were being served and I would be on in ten minutes.

"Tom," I said. "I can't stop this infernal bleeding. I'm going under the table to lie down; make a long introduction and when the bleeding stops I'll tug on your trousers."

I quietly slipped beneath the table, well hidden from the four hundred guests by a banner that masked the elevated dais. Snyder stood up for the introduction and rambled along nicely. He gave me a slight kick to get ready. The bleeding continued. He kept on kicking. I took off his loafers and then his socks. Snyder was barefooted and livid. He introduced me, ready or not.

The bleeding had stopped, fortunately, and I managed to slip up to the microphone for my speech:

". . . Wastebasket Millie is her name. She cleans up offices after hours, sells rejected ad campaigns out of trash barrels to rival agencies for five-figure sums. By day she lives on Park Avenue and owns a Rolls Royce. . . .

"Where are you going to find new low-cost media outlets to replace skyrocketing television-commercial time costs? There are several hundred thousand bald-headed men in major cities who could serve as mobile billboards with stenciled messages on their heads. . . . a great media buy for Avis, Coke, or IBM. Only five dollars an hour per baldy . . ."

At the conclusion, Snyder had to wait until the crowd cleared out before he could retrieve his shoes and socks. He left, furious. This episode was probably instrumental in keeping me off his "Tomorrow" program. I tried many times for an opportunity but was rejected by Snyder's staff.

Determined to appear on the show, I reached into my bag of tricks and pulled out "Omar the Beggar." As mentioned earlier,

Omar was just a figment of my imagination; he supposedly taught professional panhandling to unemployed executives who needed fast funds. Omar's philosophy via a press release said:

> Creative panhandling is a discreet selling style. There are no credit losses, no overhead, and very little bookkeeping. I teach a beggar how to become a proud professional.
>
> Illegal? More illegal than the millions in kickbacks to Arabs by American oil companies? Or corporate campaign-giving to political candidates under the table?
>
> Immoral? More immoral than using sex to sell merchandise in advertising? Or church-sponsored Bingo?
>
> Diabolical? More diabolical than car manufacturers substituting plastic for vital metal parts? Or the CIA using taxpayers' money to kill God knows who?
>
> You bet your ass what I'm doing is illegal, immoral, and diabolical! That's the American way of doing business. The Twentieth-Century Golden Rule is "Do unto others before they undo you!" Panhandling is the great American dream that Horatio Alger would be proud of. . . .

"Tomorrow" producer Bruce McKay couldn't ignore such an intriguing subject and Omar the Beggar was invited to appear as a guest.

In order not to reveal my true identity and risk cancellation, I donned a black hood ("to protect my anonymity among friends and relatives") and took along a hysterical wife, played by super actress Evelyn Jones, as a distraction from my disguise.

She kept pleading with me from the time we arrived inside the NBC-TV Rockefeller Center building until we entered the studio:

"Omar, don't go on the air! Think of our kids in school! Please, let's go back home. It's still not too late. Let Mr. Snyder interview Tiny Tim or Ugly George. Not you!"

Evelyn cried tearfully in full view of studio guards, the program staff, camera crews, and the audience. I also brought a personal body guard, actor Frank Murgalo, dressed in a black suit, white tie, and suspicious bulge under his left breast pocket that resembled a holstered gun.

Snyder never suspected who was really under the hood as we traded verbal punches for the full hour, leaving author Erma Bombeck stranded in the wings:

"You're a sick man, Omar!" he shouted. "Teaching panhandling is sinful; you are a disgrace to the human race!"

"You can talk," I countered, "with your six-figure salary, fancy clothes, and a chauffeured limousine. What do *you* know about being poor?"

I thought the show was my best. One television reviewer said: "It was as though William F. Buckley and Jerry Falwell stepped into the ring for a debate on pornography, beastiality, and bedwetting nonstop . . . a welcome throwback to the great old video days of Joe Pyne and Alan Burke. . . . Please do it again, Tom!"

Eventually Snyder learned about the masked man from mutual friends who just had to tell. He wouldn't believe it until I visited his office:

"The viewer reactions were fantastic, Alan," he said, "but I still can't forgive you for leaving me barefooted in Philadelphia."

Pay Now, Give Birth Later

Six months prior to the birth of our baby, I had made reservations at St. Vincent's Hospital in New York that involved a $500 deposit.

Jeanne looked like she was carrying twins on the frantic day I hovered over her with a stopwatch. After eight hours of labor pains, coming more frequently, the doctor said it was time to go. No taxi driver would pick us up and chance a delivery in his back seat; so she hid while I hailed a cab. The driver groaned, but didn't toss us out.

When we rushed into St. Vincent's, I was amazed to learn the hospital office had no knowledge of any advance payment. They demanded a check before my expectant wife would be admitted. I threw a minor temper tantrum until the security guard waved the nurse and mother-to-be-any-minute on ahead.

The obstinate office manager and I were nose to nose.

"I see no record of any deposit," she insisted.

"But I paid," I said vehemently. "You've had my money for the past six months. I can't understand this kind of sloppy bookkeeping."

I insisted upon speaking with the hospital administrator to resolve this situation. Now there were two adversaries who conducted a final but futile search for my deposit. They demanded payment or I would have to find another hospital.

In my anxious state of impending fatherhood, I had almost forgotten the canceled check was in my wallet. Out of instinct, one must expect every peak experience in life to be sabotaged; you don't learn how to thrive on rejection without going into combat forearmed.

Two very red faces examined my check. A photocopy was made and, amid profuse apologies, I took the opportunity to fire a parting salvo:

"I hope your doctors and nurses don't perform the way you people demonstrated. Furthermore, since you obviously have my money, where is it? Has it been stolen from within? Are there internal bookkeeping problems that need to be investigated by the district attorney?"

They assured me there was no cause for such action. I was given the use of a vacant office between sessions with my wife's labor pains and allowed to make phone calls.

On yes, sixteen hours later we had Jennifer. One look at that cute puckered face and Jeanne knew it was well worth all the pain. As for me, one look at them both and, like many another proud new father, I forgave the hospital for all *my* anguish.

Another Manuscript Rejected!

A series of humorous lectures I gave in Canada came to the attention of Jack McClelland, chairman of the publishing firm McClelland & Stewart. He suggested a book presentation be submitted. Instead, I finished the entire manuscript with essays ranging from social solutions to medical commentaries:

". . . your body is an antique. Aren't you bored with the human anatomy? It hasn't changed for nearly twenty thousand years, you know. Take a good look at yourself and you'll agree there's room for improvement.

"That's why I visited Denmark last month and observed Dr. Jormond Shanks's private clinic where he was busy attaching a third arm to the base of a man's spine. Made of plastic and connected to nerve centers, it functions as another limb. This particular fellow was soon eating an apple with his right hand, signing an autograph with the other, and using the third one to scratch his behind.

"All tests are being made by Dr. Shanks on human beings, rather than animals, to avoid the ire of antivivisection organizations who have threatened to picket the clinic.

"With an additional arm, a person can carry extra packages, shake hands from behind (ideal for busy politicians), or drop this extra limb to the floor as a tripod for resting on line at the bank or supermarket.

"When not in use, the arm swings up and lies flat between the shoulder blades, hardly noticed under a tailored topcoat. . . ."

There were fifty essays submitted, representing two years of trial and error, with the dubious title, *The Fallacy of Creative Thinking*.

Three months went by before publisher McClelland called from Toronto to arrange a luncheon date in New York the next day.

"Don't forget the contract," I said.

"I just might," he replied playfully.

We enjoyed an excellent lunch at a busy East Side restaurant with huge wooden round tables. McClelland and I had to bend forward to communicate.

"I just don't know how to break the news," he said, "but we're turning your book down. We don't think it will sell sufficiently; perhaps you'll find a publisher in the States."

I was truly stunned, totally unprepared for this devastating turn of events.

"It's the consensus of my sales staff," McClelland continued. "Even though I thought your ideas were extremely amusing, I don't like to interfere with their judgment."

He took my manuscript out of his briefcase and reached across the table. We were so far apart I had to stretch out to grasp it. At least there were no coffee stains or disfigured pages!

The waiter came over and handed me the check.

"Let me have that," McClelland said, reaching in vain as I held it several feet away.

"Did you ever invite an author to lunch when he or she picked up the check?" I asked.

McClelland reflected for a minute before answering.

"No, in all my publishing years I can't recall ever having an author pay when I extended the invitation."

"Well, Mr. McClelland, you've got a first in your life because I intend to pay. I see a year of writing going down the drain in this restaurant along with the dirty dishwater. So I intend to clean up the entire mess by paying the bill. And if anyone ever asks you, remember there was only *one* author who picked up the check."

He looked at me and smiled.

"You really insist, you won't let me pay?"

"Absolutely not."

"In that case, I'm going to overrule my staff and publish your book. Let me have that manuscript back."

I paid the bill, he published the book, and there were excellent reviews and sales in Canada.

It was such an incredible fluke for reversing a publishing decision, one of the reasons for smiling at misfortune and learning to thrive on rejection. While you're entitled to feel rotten when turned down, you can't run for the finish line with your tail between your legs. Paying that check was really a gesture of my frustration.

How to Throw Your Voice

Stewart, a talented newscaster friend, was dropped from a network station when economic cutbacks were ordered. Although he had seven years of loyal and efficient service, Stewart was low man on the seniority totem pole. His Christmas present was two weeks' notice and eight weeks' severance pay.

After six months of mailing resumes to the major news stations in a hundred cities, all he had to show were rejections, a few invitations to lunch "next time you're in our city," and bills for printing, postage, and long-distance telephone calls.

Stewart was worried about keeping the house, supporting a wife and two kids, and maintaining his pride. All savings had vanished and a second mortgage was hastening financial disaster.

I rode in a New York taxi one day that was driven by Stewart. He wondered if I had any suggestions towards getting hired for television commercials, particularly voice-over announcements. I promised to give it some thought and we planned a luncheon date that following week.

My wife, Jeanne, came up with a solution she had once used to gain employment as a television actress. The plan was to visit casting agents after making the required appointments. Then, in the reception area of each office, he would have a young lady in tow posing as an interviewer for *People* magazine:

"Tell me, Stewart. How do you feel about spending all day under the hot television lights perspiring for products you recommend but don't use?"

"On the contrary, Cindy. I won't make a commercial if I don't personally try and use the product. Sincerity is a must and cannot be faked. The public is very perceptive nowadays."

The reporter's questions would be answered loudly enough to be heard by the receptionist. This technique identifies his voice and provides a sample audition in the event she has to recommend a commercial announcer for an emergency replacement. It does happen.

During the agent's appointment, the interview continues with permission. It's impressive that Stewart is being profiled for a national magazine. And there wouldn't be any problem explaining why the article was never published. Magazines spend millions each year on stories that die before publication. Reporters collect more "kill fees" for abandoned interviews than they do for ones printed.

Stewart was pleased with the proposal and went into action. On his seventh interview with an agent he was hired for a network television commercial and this triggered a series of subsequent calls and assignments.

He is still working in this highly specialized and lucrative field called "voice overs." The performer is never visible, only his voice is heard. However, the income is extremely prominent, $50,000 a year and up—much better than driving a cab or owning a fleet.

The New York All-Star Nude Jazz Band

Rich Szabo is a virtuoso trumpet player–arranger, formerly with the Ray Anthony and Maynard Ferguson bands. At the ripe old age of twenty-three he organized his own big band with screaming brass and wailing reeds, reminiscent of an earlier Stan Kenton–Charlie Barnet era.

After being rejected by every major record company, Szabo raised $60,000 among musician friends and recorded his first jazz album with original tunes and swinging arrangements that compared with the best of big bands.

He sent out promotional albums to radio stations and waited for reactions. DJs wouldn't play the record because they only programed the top forty hits and their MOR (*m*iddle-*o*f-the-*r*oad) policy stayed with disco or perhaps Lawrence Welk music.

In order to induce sales, a recording must be played over and over continuously. Szabo wasn't about to receive this treatment. The record business has been around for fifty years and so has payola in one form or another. Major record companies can afford to supply DJs with free merchandize, booze, vacation trips, drugs, cash, and women. Also men, if that's their choice. The biggies write these expenses off under "promotion and entertainment." It's all perfectly legal in terms of their internal accounting procedures.

A radio disk jockey is no different from any other service employee who works for gratuities. He or she expects to be paid for services rendered. A new record client pays up front; an older one after the records begin to sell, with escalating bonuses if the sales go over a million copies.

The more discreet payments are made to record DJs' relatives, who pay taxes to Uncle Sam, take a percentage for their "laundry service," and hand over the balance to the record spinner. Sometimes the DJ and/or his relative will receive a small percentage of the publishing royalties; every record that is sold pays four cents to the publisher, who shares this with the composer. That's four cents for each song. On an album with twelve songs, it's forty-eight cents. A million albums sold means $480,000 to be split.

Then there is performance income. Whenever a tune is played on the air, one of three licensing organizations (ASCAP, BMI, or SESAC) pays the publisher and composer fees based upon a sliding scale reflecting local and national performances. For example, Paul Anka, the composer of Johnny Carson's "Tonight" show theme song, earns over $200 a night five times a week!

Hundreds of millions of dollars are paid out every year by the licensing organizations to their copyright holders. Further income is received from the sale of sheet music, from overseas licensing, and for performances in discos and night clubs where live or recorded music is featured.

This enormous bundle of money creates a very attractive golden goose and there is enough booty to siphon off a hefty portion for payola purposes.

Station managers hotly deny the existence of "record plays for pay" with the same indignation that DJs insist their musical programing represents the popularity polls. Nevertheless, recording-company executives know how to capture those polls by oiling the proper turntables.

The chance for an unknown performer to receive airplays without big bucks is nil. There are no free rides and the piper must be paid, unless you have a far-out gimmick.

When Szabo changed his band's name from the Rich Szabo Orchestra to "The New York All-Star Nude Jazz Band" and replaced the album cover with a photograph of nude musicians, this made the difference. A thousand copies went to DJs who couldn't resist the temptation to find out just what kind of music a bunch of nudists would play. They were pleasantly surprised and started to program the album. (The cover photo was staged by male models holding instruments.)

Sales materialized and Szabo receives bids for concerts beyond his wildest expectations. Bookers insist that the musicians keep their clothes on for engagements and they are only too happy to comply.

So far he hasn't played before any nudist colonies but the band might consider a performance in the raw—if the price is right.

Space Exploration

Dave Lawson graduated from Purdue University with a degree in petroleum engineering. His first job offer was for a major oil company starting at $40,000 plus travel and living expenses. The only catch: working in Saudi Arabia for three years. But the money was great—no taxes, free room and board—and this meant a nest egg for later life in the States.

Upon arriving in Riyadh, Saudi Arabia, Lawson found the private living quarters promised weren't quite what he envisioned. Rather, his cot, dresser, closet, and desk space were one of twenty other units in a dormitory! Each "private" area was separated with floor-to-ceiling draw curtains. There was no privacy at all.

Lawson wrote me he was terribly unhappy, angry, and in desperate need of personal space. He felt that the personnel recruiter had lied by assuring him he would have his own "compartment" space for living. Obviously, the definition of privacy in an Arab country was a bit different; or perhaps a misunderstanding over the words "compartment" and "apartment."

I advised him to do his job well, stay cool, and be patient. Also, he should write his family physician back home in Moline, Illinois, and explain that his work was suffering from ochlophobia (fear of crowds). And would the good doctor kindly write his boss with a strong recommendation for a private apartment immediately.

Lawson's doctor understood the situation and a proper letter was drafted.

In less than a month after he had arrived overseas, Lawson was given a seldom used VIP pad in a garden apartment, with access to a swimming pool and tennis court. He is one of the most contented and popular engineers in Saudi Arabia, particularly on weekends when both fellow workers and lovely ladies enjoy his private living quarters.

Expose Yourself on TV

Television programs display ambiguous hospitality toward guests. If you have a book rising on the charts, or you're doing something that's getting newspaper coverage, it's red carpet all the way with a classy hotel suite, gourmet meals, and limousine service.

If you've been out of newsprint for a while, you're a has-been. It's a hotel room usually maintained for maids stranded overnight; food is limited to the coffee shop; you taxi your own way to and from the studio.

Celebrities demand and receive royal treatment or they won't perform. I once offered to share my taxi with British actress-comedienne Hermione Gingold from the hotel to a studio where we were appearing on the "Mike Douglas Show." Although it was a short distance away, she refused to arrive in anything less than a chauffeured limousine. The video taping was held up until proper transportation could be arranged for her.

On a trip from New York to Cleveland with activist attorney Mark Lane for a television program, we were not allowed to board our plane. It had been oversold and our ticketed reservations were to be validated for a later flight. Lane demanded and received a private jet for the trip on *his* time schedule, not the airline's.

"Front Page Challenge" and "To Tell the Truth," two of television's longest-running shows in Canada and the States respectively, maintained an ironclad rule that no guest could ever appear more than once. However, I managed to break this stranglehold on talent by appearing repeatedly under various disguises.

The insatiable appetite of the tube quickly devours a performer's best creative juices and the talent bookers seek new prey with the tenacity of a black widow in heat. For nonstars, wearing out your welcome after one appearance is one dilemma; another is being blackballed by the competition.

For example, Johnny Carson wants exclusivity. Appearing on a rival program, even in a different time slot, is an automatic blacklist. Exceptions are made only for major stars promoting their films, shows, books, and record albums.

All television producers pursue the same dog-eat-dog attitude. In New York it's your choice of "Good Morning America" or "Today," but you can't have both. Chicago brandishes "Donahue" versus "A.M. Chicago" and in Los Angeles it's "Thicke of the Night" against any other show.

The public pays for this closed-shop mentality because mediocrity prevails as the same regulars, a small group of "in" stars, dominate our screens. New faces occasionally appear, but talk shows continue to compete for stars and virgins, nothing in between.

I've been able to overcome this objectionable rejection to television exposure for myself and others by utilizing a variety of masquerades and proposing intriguing or humorous concepts.

My favorite target has been television editorials. Station managers deliver their comments on local, state, and national issues just prior to the nightly network news. Opposing opinions are encouraged and must receive equal time under FCC and National Association of Broadcasters' rules.

Therefore, it is possible to gain valuable television exposure for writing and performing satire. Otherwise the only proving ground is some comedy club on talent night, if you're willing to appear at 4 A.M. before eight drunks and the kitchen staff.

For example, WCBS-TV in New York City mounted an editorial campaign to reduce drunken driving. Their battle cry was to throw the culprits in jail and suspend their licenses. I responded with this televised plea, posing as a slightly inebriated driver:

"Channel Two recently urged revocation of drivers' licenses who are apprehended under the influence of alcohol. Channel Two also suggested random checkpoints to catch cars with booze. Such a move violates our basic freedom under the Constitution. If we monitor the drinking driver, shouldn't we also smell the breath of airline pilots before they take off? Or high-rise construction workers tossing hot rivets around?

"Drunken drivers have fundamental problems that need to be resolved on a psychiatrist's couch. Taking away the driver's license is a hollow cry of despair against a growing sea of

inebriation. An unlicensed driver will load up on liquor and find a car to drive. Furthermore, fake licenses are a dime a dozen.

"Channel Two is putting a Band-Aid on a gaping, bloody wound. Drunken drivers are emotionally sick people who need to be cured. Let them keep their licenses but give them thirty days in Bellevue Hospital for analysis and rehabilitation. Meanwhile, park their cars along the New York Thruway with the keys in the ignition, a tank full of gas, and a map of the United States.

"There are over sixty thousand dangerous people killed yearly on our national highways; this way we take the drunks' cars away and give them to thieves who will meet their maker in a fatal accident. What better opportunity is there to whittle down the criminal population?"

Anybody can qualify for television or radio editorial airtime by submitting an opposing view to the station's manager. You'll be playing to a prime-time audience—one minute before the evening news—that is larger and more attentive than any local talk show can offer.

Furthermore, you don't need a resume, an agent, or an audition.

Delivery Guaranteed

At the height of the revelation that Hitler's diary was a hoax, writer Terry Ryan put together a spoof entitled *Adolf Hitler's Real, Authentic, Cross-my-hear-and-hope-to-die-in-a-bunker Diary.*

I suggested he make a pitch to the hundreds of publishers attending a yearly convention in Dallas. We flipped a coin and I won the trip to Texas. Only half of the diary presentations arrived; the others were stalled somewhere within American Airlines' Priority Package system.

The final shipment arrived after the convention ended, but I still had to pay the temporary employees I had hired to pass out the presentations, and other expenses. I filed a complaint against American Airlines and they rejected my demand for compensation.

"Our liability is limited to not charging you for the air freight bill, that's all," an official told me by phone.

"Baloney!" I replied. "Your entire advertising campaign stresses delivery guaranteed within hours, not days. You're either engaging in false advertising or some sort of fly-by-night scam."

He wouldn't buy that appraisal. My next stop was Small Claims Court in New York City. A sympathetic judge found the defendant guilty and ordered American Airlines to pay for "perishable printing, employees wages and incidental expenses" totaling $799.55.

Most air freight services exert every effort to deliver the same day. Your order is taken by phone at a communications center in some faraway city like Seattle or Oklahoma City. They contact a local forwarding firm for the pickup. But if the truck driver is at lunch, in traffic, or suffering from cramps, your package isn't going to be on the necessary flight.

There is a fail-safe solution. Let's say your precious parcel in New York must reach Los Angeles by midnight P.S.T. Here's how you do it.

I had a master tape that was required to be at a West Coat radio studio for a midnight airdate. After making a copy, in the event it had to be transmitted by telephone, I took a taxi to JFK Airport around 6 P.M. and stationed myself in the departure area of TWA. A flight was scheduled to leave at 7:45 P.M., arriving in Los Angeles 10:15 P.M. P.S.T.

One young chap looked as though he might be willing to earn $50 for carrying the small carton west. When I explained the circumstances, he was definitely interested and assured me his lady friend would drive the tape directly to the radio station.

We exchanged identifications and the mission was accomplished on time. I have used this method often with great success and very little cost.

American Airlines' attorney wasn't too happy over the Dallas decision and he was even more annoyed when I returned to court with another claim against his client. This one concerned a free-flight coupon signed over to me by a former friend for $150.

The only problem was I had to fly somewhere, anywhere, within three days. It suddenly dawned on me I wanted to stay home and rest for the next three days, not travel to Brazil or Hawaii, which I could have.

I used some telephone sales persuasion with American Airlines and they agreed to a ninety-day extension if I mailed back the coupon for revalidation.

Nothing happened for six weeks and American Airlines couldn't find my file. Then I called my former friend to see if he might have some information. He had just returned from a delightful trip to the Caribbean on my free pass that the airline had inadvertently returned to him. I could have my $150 back, which I declined.

When I wrote to American Airlines about the injustice of not honoring my property rights, they copped out by explaining their rules required them to deal only with the original awardee.

Small Claims Court upheld my verbal contract and the Caribbean is now on my agenda. I also have $150 back plus interest and one less name on my Rolodex file.

Living in Sin

Jack was living with Jill in Indianapolis for a year after they both graduated from college with honors. Their respective parents constantly urged them to marry and stop "living in sin." This objection to Jack and Jill's ideal arrangement bugged them. Every telephone call or letter from home ended with the familiar refrain: "You know it's not right and we don't approve."

The showdown came when Jack and Jill decided to go for their master's degrees and continue living together. But who was going to pay for the extra year of schooling?

Both sets of parents offered to supply the funds, but only if their children either married or lived separately. Jack called me in New York with his problem. He had to make a decision in two weeks or lose out on entering the fall term and an available apartment off campus.

This young couple, whom I had known for several years, just wanted peace of mind, and "getting married" was the answer.

As an ordained minister in the Universal Life Church, I offered to marry them. He was ecstatic over this solution and immediately set the wedding date for two weeks from Sunday. It was summer and they could hold the ceremony outdoors. We agreed upon a fee for my services and I was reminded to perform a Jewish wedding.

That last item threw me. Fortunately, my friend Bob Blumenblatt was well steeped in Judaism and he gave me the necessary instructions. I already had a paper yarmulke from a funeral service the previous year and an appropriate morning suit fit for a U.S. senator.

Jack and Jill's parents were delighted to hear the good news. They offered to handle all details with a posh country club in Indianapolis—except for the couple's New York rabbi friend.

Due to the sensitivity and secrecy of this mission, I decided to fly to Indiana on the appointed Sunday, arrive minutes before the ceremony, and depart for New York immediately afterwards.

When I reached Indianapolis, a limousine was waiting and Rabbi Abel arrived at the country club in style. Several hundred people stood on the spacious lawn drinking champagne as a string ensemble played Israeli folk songs. My heart fluttered at this expensive wedding that was all my fault. But there was no backing out now. On with the show!

I stood at the pulpit, muttered an unintelligible prayer in pigeon Hebrew and quickly joined the happy couple in matrimony. Jack had suggested a brief sermon; my remarks on the immorality of our present-day society brought polite applause: ". . . the Surgeon General's warning on cigarettes is a farce; instead, why doesn't he force prostitutes to wear a sign saying, 'this activity could be hazardous to your heath' . . .

". . . in spite of the Watergate scandal, a gigantic betrayal of public trust, we must learn to forgive sinful people. President Carter's brother, Billy, urinated on an Atlanta runway. We must forgive him. Pandas are mating in a Washington zoo, a public peep show attended by tourist families with binoculars and cameras. We must forgive them. . . ."

Following the ceremony, a rock band played while the guests sat down for dinner with the bride and groom. My driver had disappeared temporarily so I couldn't resist sitting in on drums with the musicians.

One elderly man came over to me as I was leaving and said, "Now I've seen everything . . . a swinging rabbi!"

"What about the Singing Nun?" I responded.

"I saw her too," he said.

Passing up the sumptuous filet mignon dinner to avoid any embarrassing questions about my synagogue, I headed back to the airport and home.

Jack and Jill lived happily ever after through their first school year and then split. Marriage didn't work out for them after all. Too bad. It probably ruined a previously good relationship.

Training a Troublesome Tyke

Becky Burns teaches music at Colonial Hills Elementary School in Worthington, Ohio. Her biggest problem used to be rebellious boys who created turmoil and upset the other students. She feared losing control of her classes if unruly fourth and fifth graders continued their rude ways.

It only takes one misfit to spoil a climate of learning in school. Accordingly, I believe Congress should federally fund personal liability insurance for teachers and grant moderate spanking rights. Especially after a kid has ignored three commands to behave.

Youngsters want to be reprimanded and guided, providing they are taught with a sense of love and understanding. Macho types on television and indifferent parents have certainly contributed to student arrogance in the classroom.

Ms. Burns first tried the usual punishment methods: having the kid wear a dunce hat, sit in the corner, go to the principal's office, or stay after school to write "I am a bad boy" one hundred times on the blackboard. In habitual cases, a warning letter was sent to parents.

None of these techniques really deterred the few incorrigibles, and a minority of overactive muppets threatened to rule. Then she applied a bold rule of practical psychology: "The next time you boys misbehave, I'm going to *kiss* you in front of the class."

Each new school term there is always one youngster who rejects her threat. She delivers a resounding kiss to the cheek and *presto*! The laughs, giggles, and jeers from both boys and girls give her total command throughout the year.

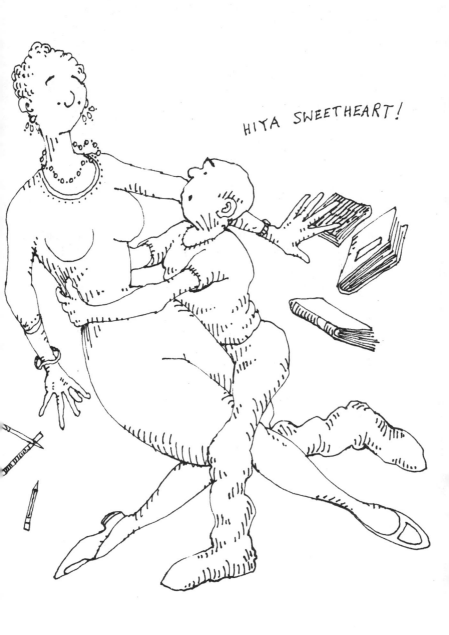

For a girl who misbehaves, Ms. Burns has a quiet chat with her after class. Little ladies tend to be pussycats until they learn the facts of life, including but not limited to financial statements, Dow-Jones stock averages, and palimony.

However, the fear and embarrassment of a young boy being kissed by his teacher in class is greater than any corporal punishment ever devised. So, teachers, try it. You'll like it!

How to Succeed, More or Less

This excerpt is from a lecture last year at Cornell University:

". . . if you go into the professional arts you're only as good as your last show, film, book, or record album. Even then, after you've paid your performance dues, you'll audition again and again. Can you imagine a doctor being asked to prove himself before doing a heart bypass operation? What would a dentist think if a patient asked him to perform an extraction on somebody else first? Or a lawyer to recite some past litigation?

"These men would have you committed for observation. So why can't the powers-to-be have the same faith in artistic talents that Woody Allen has in Mia Farrow? Or Meshulam Riklis with Pia Zadora?

"The elitist crowd in charge upholds America's supremacy in mediocrity because they simply don't know or care. Perhaps both. Some are human though. The chairman of the board of one of this country's largest corporations invited me to lunch. I arrived half an hour early, his secretary was out, and I peeked into his suite. He was on the floor playing with a toy car mumbling baby talk. That's my kind of man and we got along famously.

"Now all of you out there play with toys, talk to yourselves, maybe even play with yourselves. It's all right. You have that privilege. Just ask Dr. Brothers or Dr. Ruth Westheimer. But could the Board of Trustees allow your college President the freedom to flash during graduation? Probably not.

"Unfortunately, the totalitarian rule of your destinies is going to remain with a few families who control the company stock. Their offspring will function in the same dull, unimaginative, mentally castrated manner. The disloyal black sheep are given money and ostracized to Ibezia or Aspen. Early retirement in style.

"Where do you think all the new hotel porters, taxi drivers and dishwashers are coming from? Puerto Rico and Guatemala? Oh no, there are plenty of unemployed writers, directors, actors, singers, and dancers willing to degrade their lifestyles for survival. They're hanging in, waiting for success.

"Very few will ever make it. The doors to opportunity open with a magic word spelled on the handles: *Pull*. If you want in, your mom, dad, uncle, or cousin will have to turn a special key. It's called nepotism.

"Sounds gloomy, right? Wrong! It is possible to thrive on rejection. A millionaire friend once offered to trade lifestyles with me. I could have his real estate, Rolls-Royce, condominium, and a million dollars in cash. He wanted to live like I do, with the freedom to think and behave irrationally, having fun in life.

"I considered the swap for about three minutes. Along with all his treasures I would have to take two ex-wives on alimony, a bad back, and analysis twice a week. No thanks. I'll keep my brief periods of unemployment, my good health and happiness.

"So if you don't hitch your wagon to the almighty buck, is that wrong? No, it's bad news. You need money to survive. Do like the big companies. Diversify your holdings or talents. Learn typing, a foreign language, shorthand, word processing, get a chauffeur's license and a passport. You might end up as an assistant to Grant Tinker, head of NBC Television, or become Bo Derek's secretary. She's head of anything she wants.

"When you leave this institution, be prepared to discover that hard work and talent are not necessarily integral factors for succeeding. Important are cunning, ruthlessness, greed, luck, image, breeding, and religion. Think about this. Shall we pray? There is a question in the balcony:"

"I've spent three years majoring in communications and in less than an hour you've shattered my goals. Thanks a lot!"

"Sorry. Would you consider becoming an embalmer? The pay is excellent."

"Hasn't your life been one of deception? You've used aliases and pretended to mount various nonexistent campaigns. How do you justify *that*?"

"It's part of my arsenal of defense techniques for surviving. I like to create ideas, write satire, and perform. But the marketplace is closed to outsiders, minorities and majorities, regardless of talent or dedication. Quality is often synonymous with quackery. So why not be a phony something or other, just to attract attention? My deceptions are used to infiltrate forbidden areas, obtain acceptance, and then I perform. This lady in front has a question."

"How much money do you make?"

"Come on now, you're asking a very personal question. Did you bathe today? Did you have sex last night? When does your menstrual cycle begin? Answer mine and I'll answer yours."

"Yes, I took a bath today; no, I didn't have sex last night, and my period begins next Tuesday."

"Thank you. Might we have dinner Monday night? My income fluctuates. I never know or worry. And I believe in bartering for survival purposes. Also package deals. Presently I'm seeking an orthodontist who teaches viola for Jennifer, my eleven-year-old daughter. Thank you for your attention this evening."

Let's Sign an Ironclad Contract

True or false? Signing a contract in the presence of a lawyer is always binding. Answer: false. Question: If the agreement is executed under the laws of a foreign country, you are well protected. Answer: forget it.

My dealings with an Italian film distributor were memorable. Mario signed the papers in red ink (a definite warning signal!), paid ten percent down "with the balance to follow." I suspected there was no balance and nobody to follow.

Although he promised to cable the funds within forty-eight hours after returning to Rome, I waited in vain. Mario called from overseas two weeks later: "You only gave me ten percent of the film. Ninety percent is blank leader. What happened?"

I explained that I would send the rest when he cabled the money as promised. Mario said it was difficult to transfer funds "due to new government rulings."

It was goodbye film distributor and balance due.

Several years ago I signed a contract in Hy's elegant Toronto restaurant, surrounded by two successful television producers and their attorney. How could anything but good result from this coalition? It turned out to be costly in time, money, and friendships.

The two producers had formed a motion picture company and I was selected to write their first screenplay based upon *The Midas Compulsion*, an intriguing book about a Canadian entrepreneur trading in gold-mining stocks.

I returned to New York with a promise that my $15,000 advance would be mailed as soon as the new Frank & Sam Production Company received its checkbook. Another payment of $15,000 was due upon completion of the screenplay.

When the first check didn't arrive after a month of frenzied work, I called one of the producers and learned that a Canadian mail strike had probably trapped the check between borders.

Why worry? I had a signed contract and the people behind this project were well known in the entertainment field as was their attorney. What could possibly go wrong? Answer: everything.

The Frank & Sam corporation, hardly a fetus, was headed for an abortion. When I personally delivered the completed script to Toronto three months later, I sensed a climate of frigidity.

For starters, there was no money in the corporation to pay any bills. Then, after reading my screenplay, the producers didn't think it was right. Would I forget the whole mess for $1,500?

I refused. The offer was raised to $2,500 and stayed there as our respective attorneys saw no resolution other than going to court. This would mean years of litigation, probably followed by a $30,000 judgment against an empty bank account.

Instead, I wrote a form letter that went out to over five hundred writers, producers, and attorneys in Canada asking for moral support, and enclosing a copy of the signed contract to establish credibility and a summation of all that had transpired.

Responses poured in supporting my position and expressing abhorrence over the producers' unwillingness to honor their obligation. Some months later, my Toronto attorney, Alan Levy, called to announce a settlement in full that included interest and expenses.

Tennis, Anyone?

Frank Murgalo is a fairly decent tennis player. I say that because he can beat me every time. Actually, I got my worst licking at tennis some years ago on a Santa Monica, California, court. An elderly lady needed a partner and, as a hotshot kid with a mean forehand, I condescended to play a set. Helen Wills Moody, former Wimbledon champion, taught me humility in twenty minutes.

Murgalo's dream was to play just once during a major tournament in the USTA National Tennis Center in Queens. Since the Red Cross was sponsoring a Pro/Celebrity event in the summer of 1982, with Sonny Bono, Valerie Perrine, Penny Marshall, Bill Scanlon, Vijay Amritraj, and Ilie Nastase, I called to find out if an unknown but capable amateur could play.

"Absolutely not," the spokesman said. "No way."

"How about Prince Emir Assad?" I asked. "He's one of the wealthiest playboys in the world. Harvard educated, owns a mansion in Geneva, apartments in New York, Rome, and London."

"Prince Assad we'll accept," the tournament man said.

"And what about his partner, Count von Blitzstein?" I asked. "He has royal blood and is loaded."

"He can play too," came the reply.

With Murgalo posing as the Prince and myself as the Count, we worked out daily on a tennis court trying to improve my game. I discovered the legs go first; then the forehand, backhand, serve, and most of the fun.

On a Friday evening before the Saturday matches, we scheduled an hour of practice. A young couple were playing some very excellent tennis when we arrived and the fellow was speaking fluent German to his lady partner. I decided to offer him the Count's role:

"Pardon me sir, but I've been admiring your tennis. Would you be interested in playing a match at the Nationals tomorrow?"

Gregg Roffers, an engineer from Germany, was delighted to

accept the invitation, be known as Count von Blitzstein, and speak only German.

The next day, our tennis party included two security guards and two ladies dressed in traditional Arab garb. Murgalo wore a burnoose over his tennis outfit and the Count displayed a sash with two medals. I stayed in the background as their official spokesman.

When our limousine arrived at the tennis stadium, all eyes in the grandstand turned towards this strange entourage. Red Cross officials gave us royal treatment with private dressing rooms and lunch under a gaily decorated tent.

At courtside, the pros and celebrities exchanged whispered comments during an interview on USA Cable Television with the Prince. Count von Blitzstein was unable to speak because "he couldn't sprechen der English." Then they joined their respective professional partners, Vijay Amritraj from India and top-seeded player Bill Scanlon from Dallas.

The one-set match was a Three Stooges riot from beginning to end. Scanlon and Amritraj made countless errors, convulsed with laughter over the Prince's antics. Murgalo lost his burnoose racing to the net, he berated the umpire in the worst possible John McEnroe manner, called time out—using a football signal—to drink a glass of champagne, and mooned the crowd when they booed his overhead smash that missed the ball. Scoring became inconsequential as laughing linesmen were unable to officiate.

The Count played steady tennis and was left pretty much alone because he spoke only German. USA Cable televised their match before eight million viewers, including a postgame interview with the Prince:

"Prince Assad, how could a man of great wealth perform so badly on the tennis court?"

"Because money buys anything; mediocrity, bad taste, stupidity."

"What are your plans now?"

"Well, I would like to buy some real estate, such as Cleveland, Ohio. Then I may finance a movie in New York, if I can get Frank Perdue to play Mayor Koch."

The cable television interviewer, tennis officials, players, and the crowd took this farce quite seriously. I overheard two senior citizens talking in the stands:

"That Arab Prince must be worth millions," the woman said to her husband.

"You telling me," he replied. "Look at that expensive lining on his cape. Pure gold!"

That lining was five-and-dime-store metallic rick-rack that costumer Debbi Burdette had pasted to Murgalo's garage-sale sheet, fashioned into a burnoose.

Actress Penny Marshall of Shirley and Laverne fame requested a ride back to New York in our limousine and we obliged. However, it meant staying in character and the Prince kept her in stitches with his grandiose stories involving European royalty:

". . . Countess Renata Schamatta was a real . . . how do you say . . . fruitball. She made Zsa Zsa Gabor look like Mother Teresa. I think the *Nutcracker Suite* was named after her. . . . Not Teresa, the Countess . . . a very naughty lady; she went to midnight Mass, then left a pair of panties in the confessional box with her phone number; three priests switched collars . . ."

For Murgalo and Roffers it was a day they'll never forget. Playing on center court where the tennis greats reigned, being teamed with champions Scanlon and Amritraj, and amusing the fans was a very special Grand Slam.

During the 1983 U.S. Open tennis matches I happened to meet Bill Scanlon after his victory over John McEnroe. He not only remembered the Prince and Count well, but was still laughing.

"Tennis is a very serious game," he said. "Laughs aren't part of it. That day was hysterical and I'll always remember it."

Abstinence Makes the Heart Grow Fonder

There are ways to woo a mate after he or she has made it perfectly clear your relationship is finished.

After a week or two dying by the silent phone, assume a positive mental posture. Most important, ignore the rantings and ravings from close friends and relatives: "That affair isn't worth

losing a minute's sleep over. It was rotten all along and I could have told you so."

They should only know you've lost hours of sleep, considered suicide, or marrying anyone just for spite. The wound refuses to heal.

You must endure the cooling-off period. Just wait, fret, and keep busy. Swimming, jogging, horseback riding, tennis, or handball will be therapeutic.

During the third week of mourning, send a simple, humorous greeting card to the ex-mate. Don't sign it. The sender will be quite obvious. Wait another week and send a similar card with your name, this time suggesting you have recovered from temporary amnesia.

Dead silence from the other end, right? Try one more card, perhaps showing you sitting at the phone surrounded by cobwebs, empty soup cans, and a TV screen with the caption:

PLEASE STAND BY.

WE ARE EXPERIENCING

COMMUNICATION DIFFICULTIES.

I know you can't stand it much longer but keep your hands away from that telephone. Instead, send an envelope with the business card of a favorite restaurant where you both dined. On the back write: "For a reservation call: (your phone number)."

Wait three days. Now call with this message as soon as the phone is answered:

"Hi, this is Welcome Wagon. I understand you are looking for new and improved companionship. So perhaps I can show you how friendly and sincere we are. You're busy this weekend . . . and next . . . the following . . . the rest of your life?"

Well, you struck out. Maybe not. This last method could have spun the proper wheels and put you back into synchronization. After all it has been six weeks and abstinence does make the heart grow fonder.

Let's assume nothing worked. Now you go for the big guns. If you really want this person back in your life at all costs, you'll need your checkbook. Contact billboard rental companies and book an outdoor space near the person's place of business or home for one week. Your message should read:

DEAR_____
I WANT YOU AND I NEED YOU MORE THAN I CAN
SPEAK OR WRITE. SO THIS IS MY WAY OF SAYING
I LOVE YOU BECAUSE THE GOODYEAR BLIMP
WAS NOT AVAILABLE.

                ETERNALLY YOURS,
                (your phone number goes here)

That didn't work either? Shame on both of you! Maybe your relationship isn't such a good idea after all. Hope that some of the people who read your billboard and wished they had a lover with such imagination and money to burn will contact you.

However, if you still insist on capturing this one-and-only love in your life, it's time for a last shot and if this doesn't work, feel free to write me a nasty letter. I'll deserve it.

Arrange to have a full medical checkup and week's rest in a local hospital. Ask a close friend to call your former mate with the somber news: "I don't know how serious it is, but you should call. Here's the phone and room number."

The phone rings. Lower your voice and speak hesitantly:

"I'm really glad you called. I've been doing a lot of thinking lying here in bed. The doctor says I'm run down, lack of sleep, too much worrying; possibly more mental than physical when I collapsed last week. I think they're going to let me go home in another day or two. Perhaps we can meet at that restaurant just to talk. It could be the best medicine in the world. Saturday at eight? I'll make the reservations and pick you up."

Hooray! It worked! But don't ever tell. People have committed homicide for much less reason. If you must confess, wait until your first baby arrives. All will be forgiven.

How to Meet a Mate

Ken Ferber is a free-lance writer-publicist in New York City who likes women but doesn't have the time or money to seek them out through the normal channels: singles bars, social clubs, parties, video dating, or personal ads.

He usually works on deadlines and his frenetic schedule is not conducive to wooing and winning a heterosexual friend very successfully.

Ferber meets plenty of people in his business, but after a quick introduction and maybe one drink, he has to dash off to complete an assignment. His date balks at renewing any kind of relationship with him again.

In addition, Ferber has to travel extensively, often for six weeks to three months on the West Coast or in Europe. The few females who might understand or tolerate his lifestyle eventually settle into someone else's nest.

Ferber found the solution for maintaining a cozy series of loving affairs without getting too involved. He began to sublet his apartment:

APARTMENT SUBLET

One month. Maybe longer. Prefer responsible single female with sense of humor and references. Low rent if you water plants, feed cat, take phone messages, and forward mail. Two rooms, TV, radio, stereo. Safe building on Riverside Drive. Write Box＿＿＿.

With Manhattan's shortage of apartments, this ad hit the jackpot in replies—at least a hundred letters to screen and then evaluate for the person's handwriting and style. He is quite perceptive in being able to choose the top twenty for interviews.

Ferber always has a steady supply of new friendships. And when the well dries up, he is sure to leave on a trip requiring another ad, a few interviews, and a cozy companion who occasionally stays on for an extended live-in arrangement when he returns.

Sex in the Office

For office relationships it is necessary to be diplomatic. Pleas from a co-worker to date can be quickly terminated with this explanation: "My fiancé would never approve."

Should the ardent suitor persist, especially if it's your boss, great care must be used to keep an unattractive boor at bay. Consider this ploy:

Have a friend overseas send you a loving letter with plans for your future wedding. Place this letter on your desk with an inch of dental floss tucked inside the envelope. Then take an extra-long lunch period, leave the office a half-hour early at the end of the day, and arrive late the following morning.

During one of these three periods your pursuer will have read the letter—note absence of dental floss—and pressure should be off. If not, arrange for an escort service to provide you with a companion who poses as your future mate, is introduced around the office, and departs for overseas.

If, while dating someone, you accidently meet the office pest in public, introduce the partner as a close friend of your fiancé, "still in Europe."

There are certain objectionable people who bulldog themselves into our lives. They are crude, boring penny pinchers who carry peanut butter sandwiches on a date or go dutch treat to Burger King.

Don't be subtle with these wasters because tactfulness becomes a sign of weakness and encouragement. Be blatant and disgusting:

"Bob, I won't ever date you because you have B.O. and lousy hips. Now bug off before I kick you in the crotch!"

He'll run right home to shower, probably go on a crash diet, and certainly reek from erotic after-shave lotions. Then he'll try again:

"Monica, I think I've solved my problems. How about that date?"

"You may have solved the problems, Bob, but the answer is still no. I just don't relish the idea of catching pediculosis pubis."

Bob races to the dictionary, the shower, and the drugstore. Crabs are easy to find, even if they aren't there.

At this point he will either hate you or be terribly amused at your rejection techniques. In the latter instance I would give him a date. Anyone with a real sense of humor is difficult to find these days.

An overzealous female can be dealt with by explaining you're separated from a fiendish wife who has a private detective on your tail; anybody you date is bound to be photographed and hailed into court for the pending divorce trial. You wouldn't want an innocent person to be unjustly accused and scandalized in local newspapers.

Also, you can pretend you're gay, have herpes, or are an

hermaphrodite. But I wouldn't use any of these unless there is going to be a lot of geographical distance between you and the hot harlot. Otherwise, the word spreads and you'll soon beome fair game for gays or some freak dying to peek at two sex organs. There'll be no more privacy in the men's room.

Thou Shalt Not Park

Finding a parking space in any major city is like finding a job. You have to be right there when someone pulls out. Otherwise somebody else moves in. There are just too many automobiles for city streets and too few parking spaces to accommodate but a fraction of those drivers wanting to park.

Anthony van Tullekin, an industrial designer in London, works at home and manages three young boys as well. His dwelling is a four-story Victorian town house that still retains the charm and beauty of an earlier world.

Perhaps this explains why people park in front of his house, blocking the driveway, even though his Volvo station wagon is quite visible and trapped by the illegal parker. He is unable to drive out for required meetings, and even if the doors of the parked car are unlocked, honking its horn only wears the battery down. Then he has a disabled car and an irate owner to contend with.

Blowing his own horn would accomplish the same and annoy the neighbors considerably. In London, auto horns are for emergency use only and this attitude is widely respected.

Motorists continued to ignore van Tullekin's prominent sign at curbside:

> THIS IS PRIVATE PROPERTY AND PARKING IS
> RESERVED EXCLUSIVELY FOR THE OWNER.
> THANK YOU FOR PARKING ELSEWHERE.

He also tried flyers on the offenders' windshields asking them to refrain from parking there again—and, when the same driver repeated the offense, window stickers that were extremely difficult to peel off. Nothing seemed to deter free-loading parkers.

One fine day he found the solution. Van Tullekin constructed a

very realistic portable fire plug. That prop goes out early in the morning and stays on the sidewalk all day long. It successfully deters anyone from parking within thirty feet.

Van Tullekin now has two of them. The other one is loaned to friends for occasions when he and his wife are joining them for dinner and will be arriving late at the restaurant. The friends find two parking places and plant the fake plug. That empty space will be waiting for the van Tullekins when they arrive.

The driving public may not respect property rights when it comes to parking their autos, but they won't risk a stiff fine or a padlocked metal boot on their wheel by parking anywhere near a fire plug.

Another Contract, Another Crisis

Murray was a sidewalk magician in New York who dazzled pedestrians with his sleight of hand. He did rather well with cash contributions too. I thought Murray deserved a break in films and offered him a cameo role as part of a documentary.

He accepted and we agreed on a fee of $750 for a day of shooting inside an off-Broadway theater. His scene involved an audience and a dozen people on stage.

On the morning of the filming, Murray arrived with his newly acquired manager, who was also an attorney. They had a contract for me to sign and Murray's fee had been upped to $7,500! I was to agree or the show wouldn't go on.

His new fee was equal to my entire budget for the day's shooting costs; there was no way I could meet this demand. The manager left the one-page contract with me and said he would telephone Murray in an hour.

"Remember," he said on leaving, "you're dealing with a guy who is going all the way to the top, a big star in the making and you found him first. But no pay, no play."

I was furious over this backhanded turn of events and also stymied. Even if I canceled the scene, our supporting cast and crew would have to be paid. They stood around waiting for a decision, Murray sat sheepishly in his dressing room, and I decided to take a walk.

As I passed by a typewriter store an idea formed immediately. The clerk inside allowed me to use a typewriter that matched the contract, and I retyped the exact wording on similar paper, substituting $750 for $7,500, and made two copies.

Back to the theatre on the double. It was 9:45 A.M. and Murray's wheeler-dealer agent-lawyer would be calling.

"O.K. Murray, you win," I said with resignation, dropping the contract on his dressing room table. "Let's both sign and go to work."

We did and the production went on without further mishap. However, several days later I received a call from the agent-attorney. He was so hot I had to hold the phone a foot away as he raved nonstop.

When he finally ran out of steam I responded resolutely: "You played dirty pool. If that's the way you do business, fine."

I hung up, satisfied that this rejection game had been resolved in the spirit of foul* play.

How to Play with Playboy

Playboy's movie theater on Fifty-seventh Street in New York offered an open-end engagement for the world premiere of our satirical film, *Is There Sex After Death?* featuring Buck Henry. My associate producer, Michael Rothschild, and I were grateful for debuting this R-rated comedy at an established location.

We signed a contract that stipulated our being evicted from the theatre only if weekly box office grosses fell below $8,000. In that unfortunate event, two weeks' notice would be given by the theater management.

Opening night, I hired seventy-five unemployed actors and actresses to stand in line four hours before the show. This gave the passing public a sense of the film's success prior to the critics' reviews.

For additional insurance, our opening featured the steady arrival of celebrities every fifteen minutes by limousine, complete with a giant searchlight and public address announcements: "Is

*Pun intended.

that Jane Fonda arriving? Could that be Dustin Hoffman? Fred Astaire? Dolly Parton? Burt Reynolds?''

The celebrities were look-alikes. They exited the limousine to cheers and applause, made their way into the theater, went out a rear exit, and met the same limousine for another arrival. Free coffee, tea, and cocoa were served to the people milling around outside the theater who began forming a line at the box office.

The next day we enjoyed unanimous critical approval in the press, on radio, and television. Every reviewer was pleased and *The New York Times* headlined its glowing report with: ''The only really funny movie since Woody Allen's 'Bananas.' '' That assured us of a long run.

After the first six weeks of selling out evening shows in the six-hundred-seat theater, manager Steve Kutner dropped a bombshell announcement. We had to get out in two weeks, as Playboy Enterprises intended to renovate the theater in preparation for the debut of Roman Polanski's film *Macbeth*, a multimillion-dollar production of theirs.

Hugh Hefner's secretary told me they had anticipated our lasting a week or two at the most. When Hefner read the great reviews aboard his private jet, he was overwrought at Playboy's dilemma.

''What about our contract guaranteeing an endless run?'' I asked Kutner.

''Sorry,'' he said. ''We need the theater and you can easily move to the East Side, which I have already arranged. Cinema II is better located than we are.''

Rothschild and I refused to budge. Our theater grosses were topping $30,000 a week and climbing steadily. We didn't want to interrupt any momentum at the box office.

Nevertheless, Playboy began their renovations. During the day, jackhammers tore up the basement and a crew of eighteen workers used hammers, saws, and axes in a crescendo of new-construction noises. Customers angrily fled the theater demanding and receiving their money back.

Our attorney, Robert Schwartz, obtained a restraining order denying the workmen access to the theater during film showings. I served the document on the crew chief and he calmly tore it up, saying: ''You're dealing with Playboy, a billion-dollar empire.

They can buy and sell judges like McDonald's hamburgers." Then he and his men went back to work while I helped refund patrons' money.

That evening I took a long walk up Broadway to think out this crisis. Attorney Schwartz urged another court appearance involving contempt; but that would only impose fines, easily paid by Playboy, give them grounds for eviction when our grosses fell below $8,000, and entitle us to a civil suit that would take years to litigate.

Meantime, a successful film would go right down the drain. Moving to another theater meant an expensive new advertising campaign and loss of business—and time was now running out. Cinema II wanted an answer within forty-eight hours.

I passed a construction site during my frustrating walk and noticed a sign posted in bright red: "These premises protected by German Shepherd attack dogs under the supervision of Captain R. J. Ross." The Captain listed a phone number and I called. He was happy to supply me with four dogs and four armed uniformed guards when I explained the need to protect some property for a few hours the following morning.

This entourage met me at 7 A.M. the next day, an hour before the construction crew's arrival. I gave the guards their instructions and we waited.

Promptly at 8 A.M. the workers assembled and began unpacking heavy construction equipment. I handed another copy of the restraining order to the same crew chief. He threw it back and said, "We're going on overtime today, so you take this crap and shove it!"

"Before you begin," I said, "I have one brief announcement."

The men had been eying the dogs and guards with a bit of apprehension as I continued:

"This is still my rented theater, my property, and you are all trespassing. Therefore, I have taken the liberty of protecting these premises by hiring killer dogs to protect this theater from any further noise. These dogs are trained to attack and kill anyone making sounds louder than one hundred decibels. I have authorized the guards here to release the dogs when your construction begins and I will personally take full responsibility for anyone who is maimed or killed in the process. Let me warn you.

Do not attempt to defend yourselves against these vicious animals. That will infuriate them. And if you happen to kill one of the dogs, there is a $10,000 cost to replace the animal. They are all Vietnam veterans and can split a man's throat in three seconds. Then they go for the genitals."

As the guards stood grimly at parade rest and stared straight ahead, the four dogs growled beautifully, their mouths foaming slightly. The crew stood frozen. Even their breathing was muffled. One man gingerly laid down his jackhammer and tiptoed up the stairs. The others quietly followed. Nobody said a word. There was absolute silence. When everybody had left I gave a sign to remain quiet and went upstairs.

Outside the theater I noticed the crew and their leader in a huddle, whispering. It was a dramatic episode of fear and anger, but they were being extra careful not to excite those dogs! The workmen decided to go home, leaving their tools and lunch boxes behind. They weren't going to mess around with foaming four-legged fiends.

At 10 A.M. three Playboy attorneys arrived along with theater manager Kutner. They all spoke at once in animated but subdued voices, apparently having been alerted about the dogs and their special talents.

I had summoned attorney Schwartz and he showed up with another lawyer, Mervin Hecht, a partner with Roger Diamond's California law firm, to help negotiate. Both sides decided to spend the rest of the day hammering out some sort of settlement.

By that evening, in time for our sold-out house, we agreed to move to Cinema II within two weeks. Playboy would pay all expenses, including any losses and a full-fledged advertising campaign to announce the changeover.

Under the circumstances, it was an offer no producer could afford to refuse.

Betty Boop for President

For many years, Betty Boop was a favorite cartoon character with a loyal following. However, her position in the marketplace during recent times had been challenged by Snoopy, the Muppets, and the Smurfs.

This situation changed dramatically when I created a "Betty Boop for President" campaign in 1980 that was financed by vested interests in her merchandising potential.

Actress Victoria D'Orazi played the title role because she looked and sounded a bit like the original Ms. Boop. Her supporting cast included a six-piece Dixieland band led by renowned jazz clarinetist Artie Baker, and a dozen dancers, singers, and entertainers.

Betty Boop's platform became an instant success with the news media:

1. Take congressmen off salary and put them on a straight commission basis.
2. Sell ambassadorships to the highest bidders.
3. Place a suggestion box on the White House fence.
4. Transform the Capitol Rotunda into a roller-disco.
5. Draft all congressmen *first*, for infantry duty.
6. To erase the post-office deficit, print Bo Derek's photograph on postage stamps.
7. Raise the marriage license fee to $500 to eliminate uncertainty.
8. Install a lie detector in the White House and truth serum in the Senate drinking fountain.
9. Sell the gold in Fort Knox and replace it with bituminous coal to back our money reserves.
10. Base personal income taxes on body weights, with the entire family paying $2 a pound per person.

Our entourage journeyed to Atlanta for a news conference and tried to enter the patriotically decorated "Boopmobile" motor home in their Memorial Day Parade. The police wouldn't let us without a permit, so we found a side street and drove right into line between the marching bands.

Then it was on to Los Angeles for a confrontation with former President Richard M. Nixon at the Beverly Hilton. The local press covered this event with some chagrin because Mr. Nixon turned out to be a look-alike actor, Jim Dixon.

Our Mr. Nixon was mobbed by well-wishers in the hotel lobby and he had difficulty reaching his limousine when excited citizens requested autographs and conversation.

Betty Boop managed to star again in Las Vegas at the Imperial Palace hotel for a week of campaigning. Denver was another stop with a downtown parade, and we reached Detroit in time for the Republican National Convention.

By following Ronald Reagan, George Bush, and former President Gerald Ford into the Joe Louis Arena, our presence was documented on television and noticed by the thousands in attendance. We also attracted a dozen Secret Service agents who surrounded us and attempted to block the television coverage:

"You want us to leave?" I asked the agent in charge. "We're American citizens, not aliens. You can't throw us out!"

"Out, now!" the gruff-looking agent repeated.

"Could we play the 'Star Spangled Banner' before leaving and perhaps have a cigarette if you're going to shoot us?" I requested.

"Absolutely not!" the agent thundered, reaching the end of his patience.

I gave the signal for an about face and we left with our band playing "Onward, Christian Soldiers" as the audience applauded and assumed we were part of the Republican entertainment.

Later that night, several of us appeared on an all-night talk show over WXYZ-Radio to complain about the lack of hospitality by Republican forces. Betty Boop sobbed convincingly in her high-pitched voice and said: "The Secret Service looked like Doberman pinschers in tuxedos and they acted as badly. Would they throw Santa Claus out like they did me? Or Mickey Mouse? If Mr. Reagan is listening, we actors and actresses running for president should be treated like humans. We're very sensitive people."

The finale to this national publicity campaign was our own

convention at the Monarch Ski Lodge in Garfield, Colorado, where we officially nominated Betty Boop as an independent lady candidate for president of the U.S.A.

All this hoopla created numerous Betty Boop licensing contracts for imprinted merchandise, the theatrical release of a full-length feature film, a television miniseries, and a Broadway musical in the planning stage.

Miss Piggy and her companions found another contender in the ring and there always seems to be plenty of room. Otherwise, how could anyone explain the phenomenal success of Strawberry Shortcake or Cabbage Patch dolls?

Brother, Can You Spare a Dime? (I have to call my broker.)

The nice thing about panhandlers is that they usually say "please" and "thank you." White-collar criminals don't bother with manners; they just grab the money and laugh all the way to their banks.

One area of thievery extremely attractive to white collars is the movie business, especially at the theater box office. Admissions are always in cash and it takes only two people—the cashier and ticket taker—to rob management blind.

I produced a film grossing thousands of dollars weekly with $400 missing each night. The tickets sold matched the amount of money collected; but, somehow, $400 disappeared. I knew because I was counting the theater patrons.

The Amazing Randi, a professional locksmith–magician, was hired to solve the crime. He discovered the scam in five minutes. The cashier palmed fake tickets from a hidden roll while pretending to punch up legitimate ones. Her ticket-taker partner pulled out the phony tickets at the end of the evening and they kept the corresponding amount of money.

At $400 a night they were sharing $2,800 each week! Not bad for a job with a weekly base salary of $185, Blue Cross, and two weeks' paid vacation.

Their scheme had lasted seven weeks. They were fired and the theater management paid for the losses without pressing charges, to avoid bad publicity.

Just like the end-of-the-season resort area business fires, some theaters with turnstiles for admission look forward to an occasional robbery at gun point. After the thief has escaped with a few hundred dollars, the turnstile is spun several thousand times, the police are called, and the insurance-money bonanza is collected.

Another area of thievery in films is among distributors and video pirates. Even though the latter now face stiff federal penalties, the rewards amounting to hundreds of thousands of dollars are attractive to while-collar criminals.

In one instance, a major corporation asked to screen one of my film prints for a client. Subsequently, video copies showed up in their employees' library. Proving piracy would have been extremely difficult since the company only borrowed the film and couldn't be blamed for unlawful duplications unless the tapes were sold.

Another rip-off occurred upstate New York when a crooked entrepreneur set up his videotape mail order business from a stately Victorian home in Nyack. He did very well because there were no licensing fees paid for his videotapes lifted from stolen movie prints.

I had received a list of the bootleg films available in Nyack and there were several of mine boldly advertised at cut rates. My first step was to call the man, named Bernie, and ask for royalties due. He promised to put a check in the mail immediately:

"Just an oversight. Don't worry about it. You'll get your money."

"Well, that's just fine," I said. "I'm not as worried about it as Sheik Abdul Korsani is. He financed our films. And he comes from a country where fingers, hands, arms, and legs are severed for stealing."

"You can't call an oversight stealing. The check is practically in the mail."

Six more phone calls and four weeks later the check hadn't arrived. It was time for a personal call. I wore an Arab costume and, with two friends as bodyguards, went up to Nyack in a rented limousine. Our driver was in a grey chauffeur's uniform that came with the Cadillac.

Bernie, a version of Clark Kent, was visably shaken by this unexpected visit.

"Please your highness," he stammered. "I don't want any trouble from you, the police, or the PLO. The check is going out right now or I'll give it to you."

"Just put everything due in the mail," I ordered. "And by the way," I asked on leaving, "do you ever receive one of those letter bombs instead of an order?"

An $1,100 check arrived three days later. My thank-you note the following week was returned with a post office notice: ADDRESSEE MOVED. NO FORWARDING ADDRESS AVAILABLE.

Film distributors can be even more blatant money stealers; the opportunities are greater. Their percentage commission "off the top" embodies a wide range of abuses that are absorbed by theater customers: ads never placed, extra prints not ordered, and inflated expense vouchers. We pay through the nose at the box office and through the mouth at the candy and soft-drink counter.

I discovered discrepancies with one large Chicago distributor's reports when I spot-checked his suburban theaters. Posing as an usher, I wore a tuxedo and carried a flashlight. Nobody ever challenged me or suspected this older-looking trainee was really counting the house.

Irving, the distributor, had lopped off fifty percent in his reports. Presented with my figures he merely shrugged and said, "So, go ahead and sue. You'll never win because it's your word against mine. And it will cost you a bundle to lose the case."

Such audacity! Other film makers I spoke with complained about not receiving their fair share of box office receipts. Jim Blake, a California producer, told me: "You're getting fifty percent of something which is a lot better than one hundred percent of nothing, which I just received."

Blake, a graduate of Brown University, made his first feature film, entitled *The Contest*, which received rave reviews and was shown in theaters throughout the country. When he found himself head over heels in lawsuits to recover funds from distributors, Blake entered UCLA Law School and recently graduated with honors. He has another film project in one hand and a briefcase in the other filled with blank court documents at the ready.

Wearing a messenger's uniform, I visited Irving's office near closing time and delivered several packages of movie stills to a publicity aide. On the way out I spotted an empty office with a closet. That's where I hid until everyone went home.

An hour later I had Xeroxed key documents that warranted criminal indictments. The only interruption to my spying was a cleaning woman who assumed I was working overtime.

The next day I mailed copies of my evidence to Irving:

Dear Irving:

I've decided not to sue as you suggested. The enclosed documents were furnished to me by a disgruntled former employee of yours. You'll notice that these figures are fifty percent *higher* than the box office statements you furnished. Would you care to make up the difference within forty-eight hours by certified check?

Yours very truly,
Alan Abel, Producer

Irving sent a bank draft by Federal Express to New York. He knew I could have taken my evidence to the district attorney and obtained a criminal indictment. But until I produced it, he'd refused to pay. That's the way some people do business.

Remedial Rejections

When you're crossing a street after enduring gridlock, impatient motorists turning the corner will attempt to run you down. They're bigger and stronger than you but don't be intimidated. Keep moving with your head down; pretend you don't see the oncoming automobile. However, maintain a watch out of the corner of your eye in case the driver is diabolical. Then be prepared to bolt for your life. Meantime, don't look up. If the horn blows, look dumbly the other way and keep walking.

*   *   *   *

A merciless creditor calls you at home and rejects your plea to stop calling. Collection agencies thrive on threatening and embarrassing a debtor into paying promptly. To avoid the phone calls, explain that you are having difficulty with your telephone; then, in the middle of a sentence, disconnect the line. When the phone rings again, do the same thing. It will take about four disconnects to get the message across you are not a person to be abused.

*   *   *   *

You're invited to an annual party and it's always a dreadful bore, a complete waste of time. There's never enough liquor, the toy sandwiches are soggy and unappetizing, everybody stands around waiting for something to happen, and it's wall-to-wall uninteresting people.

If you can't reject the invitation on political grounds, plan for a hasty and stealthy departure. This is accomplished by arriving late, planting your coat under the bed or on the dresser (so it can be quickly retrieved), then mingling with the host or hostess and a few guests.

Make a complete circle around the party rooms, drink in hand, face smiling, feet moving clockwise. Gradually work your way back to the bedroom for your overcoat—in summer there's never a problem—and slip out the front door.

The whole process shouldn't take more than half an hour. Your presence will be remembered but you'll never be missed.

Mission to Moscow

During a recent Moscow Film Festival, I mischievously entered a ten-minute documentary spoof of Olympic events entitled "The International Sex Bowl." Actors and actresses, posing as couples from various countries, pretended to compete for climax before a black-tie audience, a panel of celebrity judges, a referee, and a spirited announcer on stage.

In order to bypass customs censorship on both sides, I retitled the entry *Separating the Birds from the Bees* and sent the film by air mail. It was insured for $200 with a return receipt requested.

The Moscow Film Festival acknowledged the film entry by letter, including an official form signed by the festival organizer, Inna E. Kisseleva. My return receipt also came back properly executed.

When the festival was held a few weeks later, press reports in the States made no mention of *Separating the Birds from the*

Bees. Nor did the title appear in their printed film program I obtained from a tourist friend visiting Moscow at that time.

After several months I wrote to the Moscow Film Festival office requesting that the film be returned. And I wrote regularly for another six months until this response arrived:

Dear Mr. Abel:

In reply to your letter I would like to inform you that the film you mention in your letter has never been received by the programmation section of the VIIth International Film Festival in Moscow; therefore it would have been very difficult to use or display it, as you have put it in your letter.

Sincerely,
Inna E. Kisseleva
Executive Director

When my tourist friend who spoke Russian called Ms. Kisseleva from New York, she denied knowing about the film or having had any correspondence whatsoever with me!

Next step, claiming the $200 insurance from the United States Postal Service. The postal authorities made their own investigation and a year later advised me that "on the basis of evidence from Moscow, yours notwithstanding, *Separating the Birds from the Bees* may have been sent and possibly returned by the respondents. Therefore, we are unable to authorize an insurance payment."

Only after I threatened to take my evidence to Small Claims Court did the post office back down and agree to pay for the film's loss.

Can you imagine the use that slice of American decadence is receiving in KGB screening rooms? I also have a very good reason for not ever including Moscow in my overseas travel plans.

Crooked Teeth

One of my teenage inhibitions was having crooked teeth. I envied the toothpaste-ad smiles of classmates and managed to keep my mouth shut during high school years. An inferiority complex over uneven uppers constantly plagued my personality.

I attended one junior-class party in a Ku Klux Klan costume and could hardly see through the hood. But everyone shouted my name immediately when they saw those jagged teeth!

Fellow students Andy Hay and Howard Shaw had fabulous smiles. So did Betty Anders and Liz Kinkley. Their winning teeth said it all and they were the popularity kids in school.

Attractive teeth are integral to success. Consider the men involved with former President Nixon. They all had beautiful smiles: Haldeman, Ehrlichman, Dean, Mitchell, Colson.

During the forties our family couldn't begin to pay for braces. There were other priorities like food, clothing, the mortgage, and buying war bonds. In retrospect, if our government hadn't been so busy developing the atomic bomb and instant coffee, we might have overcome the high cost of orthodontics.

Stanley Cox sat behind me in school. A very quiet person, he too had a few uneven teeth and it's reassuring to remember that the senior-class prophet didn't think we would accomplish much in life. When Stanley and I last met during the late seventies, his Cox hotel chain included the Biltmore and Roosevelt hotels in New York.

Thirty years of self-consciousness about my teeth came to an end when I met Dr. Irwin Smigel, a pioneer craftsman in the field of cosmetic dentistry. He said he needed only ten hours and four appointments to change my personality. And the decimal point in my savings account.

Well he did it and the result was quite dramatic. I couldn't believe the mirror. Somehow, I fear I will return to my own sulking self at the stroke of every midnight. Not so. Thanks to Dr. Smigel's marvelous bonding techniques, I continually brighten untold lives. Mailmen, sanitation workers, airline stewardesses, and taxi drivers receive my smile.

Now if I could only do something about my floppy ears, sagging shoulders, and extended hips, even Paul Newman wouldn't be all that intimidating.

S.A.T. for Doctors

I found it a bit disconcerting to visit my doctor's office and be handed a form requesting invasive personal information such as my job, income, and next of kin. Since I had been a faithfully paying patient for five years, I decided to reciprocate.

TO: All medical people
FROM: Patients and concerned citizens
RE: A review of your expertise

Please answer all questions accurately. Information will be kept on file and made available only under the guidelines suggested by the Freedom of Information Act.

1. How do you feel physically?_____
   Mentally?_____
2. Has your technique improved or deteriorated over the past four years?_____
3. What was your accumulative college grade average?_____
   Medical school grade average?_____
4. Give an opinion of yourself as a doctor:_____
   As a person:_____
5. On a scale of 1 to 10, how do you rate among your staff?_____ Among your patients?_____
6. Do you plan on raising fees this year?_____ Lowering them?_____
7. Do you accept referral kickbacks?_____ Why?_____
8. In lieu of a fee would you accept a bartering arrangement?_____ Food stamps?_____
9. Indicate your income for last year:
   _____ $50,000–$100,000
   _____ $100,000–$150,000
   _____ $150,000–$200,000
   _____ Over $200,000
10. Have you had to defend a malpractice suit in the past year?_____

11. Give an example of one of your outstanding procedures or operations:_____

12. Describe a procedure or operation that failed:_____
    Fate of patient:_____

13. If you could start your life over again, what would you really like to do?_____

14. Would you recommend that a young person interested in medicine become a:
    _____ Doctor
    _____ Dentist
    _____ Veterinarian
    _____ Malpractice lawyer

15. Do you make house calls?_____ Why not?_____

16. How would you like your tombstone to read?_____

Kids Say the Darnedest Things!

A Canadian television talk show in the late seventies was hosted by actor-comedian Paul Sholes and broadcast nightly for ninety minutes. It was CBC-TV's attempt to unseat their opposition, Johnny Carson's "Tonight" show.

Everybody takes pot shots at Carson's longevity. One rival program in Canada spoofed "Tonight" by showing him and sidekick Ed McMahon still doing their show in the year 2025 from Forest Lawn Cemetery.

"Tonight" was too firmly entrenched in Canadian homes and Sholes's "Canada after Dark" couldn't last. During the final week before its cancellation I was invited to appear and I insisted on bringing along my daughter, Jennifer, then eight, to tell a few jokes and gain some experience. The producer was reluctant to accept this arrangement.

Since she had her bag packed for several days I took her along anyway. Unfortunately, the show ran out of time when Jennifer was quickly introduced as a youngster who ate nothing but hair sandwiches because hair is high in protein, and this represented a solution to future food shortages.

"Go in any barber shop and sweep up lunch," she said.

Host Paul Sholes hurriedly cued her to tell a joke as the credits were already rolling over the final minute. The way we rehearsed, she was supposed to ask:

"Where does the Lone Ranger take his garbage?"

"I don't know, where?"

(*To the tune of the* William Tell *Overture*) "To the dump, to the dump, to the dump, dump, dump."

Jennifer was a bit flustered by the "hurry up" signals, several hundred people in the studio audience, and blinding television lights.

"Where does the Lone Ranger take a dump?" she blurted out.

Sholes fell off his chair in a fit of hysteria, the audience was convulsed with laughter, and I turned red, white, and blue as the show ended.

All across Canada a few million people witnessed what seemed to be the start of an off-color joke by a child, taught by the kid's dirty old man. Jennifer was unaware of her goof and its implication. She learned very quickly!

Don't Make Plans

World War III won't allow time for a military draft or gas rationing. Nor will there be any need for bomb shelters. Life will end in a matter of minutes, perhaps an hour, day, or week at the most.

It shouldn't take a television program like "The Day After" to remind us that survivors of a nuclear holocaust fare worse than those who perish instantly.

I attended a discussion on this subject with a group of concerned people including doctors, therapists, attorneys, and a New York state supreme court judge.

The occasion was a gathering of friends and associates of the renowned psychiatrist Dr. Irving Salan, in his Park Avenue apartment. Dr. Salan maintained this open-house forum for fifteen years until his retirement recently.

When my opinion was invited, I said simply: "Don't make plans. You think it can't happen? It will. Some dummy will fire a salvo out of fear, frustration, or just plain stupidity. There are a lot of looney Bremers, Chapmans, Hinckleys, and Sirhans who would love to play Dr. Strangelove. Don't overlook Arafat, Qaddafi, Khomeini, and even Castro. They want to take the world with them when they go. So live one day at a time . . . fully . . . and don't make any long-range plans."

On a more optimistic note, I mentioned Allan Simpson Jr., a former journalist and assistant to Congressman Ralph Regula. Simpson recently resigned his position to devote full time to expediting nuclear disarmament. His dedication is unique and out of step with Washington associates who would never trade power for preservation. Simpson has researched and written an extensive report on ways to neutralize and halt the arms race, entitled "The Prescription," that he is turning into a book.

Dr. Salan's meetings were generally quite serious, although on occasion I disrupted the solemnity. Comic Bob Pagani, a former Madison Square Garden guard, arrived one evening in uniform to announce he was looking for illegal aliens rumored to be hiding in the building. The guests were fooled for about a minute until they noticed my smirk.

Another friend, TV performer Pat Paulsen, posed as a pathological psychotic in search of a traveling therapist who would take his couch on one-night engagements. After a few minutes of jovial banter, his face and style were recognized.

When Dr. Salan was program chairman for an annual convention of psychiatrists in New York, I was hired to speak, posing as a former CIA agent who had resigned to write a book. Several hundred therapists listened intently to my ramblings at the Excelsior Club:

". . . We're CIA but we're human. Sure, I'd like to punch Ralph Nader in the nose. . . . Jane Fonda's worse, so anti-American at times. When she was against the gook war in Nam we tried to poison her. But she never ate in restaurants and we couldn't get inside her bag of fruits and nuts. Liberace was another CIA thorn. We didn't like the way he flaunted those sissy costumes. It hurt the American macho image . . . so one of our guys volunteered to tune his piano, but the tuner turned out to be gay! I see you all sitting there, analyzing me. . . . I know I need therapy, only I can't afford it now that I'm unemployed. For a while, I traded weekly trumpet lessons to a shrink for an hour on his couch. Then, at the age of forty, he dyed his hair pink, gave up a busy practice, and joined a punk rock band. . . ."

When Dr. Alvin Yapalater finally interrupted to expose the gag, there was a sigh of relief from the audience. They had been quite convinced I needed all the help I could get; none would have wanted me for either a patient or a trumpet teacher.

Howard Hughes: This Is Your Life!

My air flight from Toronto was delayed and we arrived in Vancouver well after midnight. The Bayshore Inn had rented my reserved room and I stood by the desk at 1:30 A.M. declaring war against Canada.

The desk clerk, a student, was aware of my scheduled lecture at the University of British Columbia and decided to rent me a forbidden eighteenth-floor suite at the single rate. I promised not to tell.

The lobby was full of drowsy journalists waiting for a peek at the elusive Howard Hughes, who was holed up on the entire nineteenth floor. His plainclothes security people were in the elevators, also patrolling corridors and stairwells. My suite had a terrace overlooking the bay and I could hear the Hughes entourage partying above.

An article in the *Vancouver Sun* mentioned that Hughes intended to resume movie making and was searching for a good script. How fortuitous! I had written a horror film treatment, "Who's Going to Bite Your Neck, Dear, When All of My Teeth Are Gone?" Why not toss it on his balcony with a note? I did.

Dear Mr. Hughes:

If you don't like this script, just throw it back. How about lunch tomorrow? You have to eat, you know. I have no communicable diseases and I'll wear gloves.

Sincerely yours,
Alan Abel, Suite 1805

My package had landed on the first throw with a string tied to my railing in case I missed. The next day I found only the string dangling. Somebody had acquired the script.

Following my evening lecture at the university, I joined Bob Newhart on an all-night radio talk show with host David Abbott. We discussed the Hughes mystique and I made a direct plea to him to consider my script for his next motion picture film.

Further inquiries at the hotel desk concerning all the activity on the nineteenth floor brought no response from employees. They were playing deaf and dumb. Hughes's security guards maintained stoic facial expressions and would only reply "I do not know, sir" to any questions:

"Pardon me, Mr. Guard, do you have the time?"

"I do not know, sir."

"How do you like Vancouver?"

"I do not know, sir."

"Your fly is open."

"I do not know, sir."

I returned to New York without a word from the Hughes camp and they still had my script. After another six weeks waiting for a reply, I decided it was time for assertive action.

My merry band of pranksters included an interesting group of people. Michael Rothschild was editor of *Circus* magazine; Dr. Ronald Schwartz, a urologist at Mt. Sinai Hospital; Robert Swan managed the orchestra at Radio City Music Hall; Norman Forest, a violist, played with that prestigious symphony, as did Jack Schnupp, a trombonist, and John Bartlett, a tuba player. Milt Shefter, a television writer-director, and Evelyn Jones, an actress, completed the ensemble.

We all assembled at the St. Regis Hotel's Presidential Suite to rehearse our roles. Sasch Rubinstein, a confederate in California, sent telegrams to the New York news media from Long Beach, where Hughes's flying boat, *The Spruce Goose,* was housed. Each wire read:

> I WILL BE IN NEW YORK FOR TWENTY MINUTES MONDAY AT NOON IN THE ST. REGIS HOTEL'S PRESIDENTIAL SUITE. ACCREDITED MEMBERS OF THE WORKING PRESS ONLY ARE TO BE ADMITTED.
>
> H. HUGHES

Monday morning, starting at 8:00 A.M., the St. Regis Hotel resembled a scene from a Pirandello play. Radio reporters, cameramen, journalists, lighting crews, and sound men jammed the downstairs lobby, all elevators, and the hallway leading to our suite. We had also hired four plainclothes security guards, two Pinkerton men in uniform, and four hotel employees to maintain order. They were helpless against the onslaught of media men, women, and equipment.

I played Hughes wrapped in bandages from head to toe, sitting in a wheelchair, surrounded by guards, a doctor, and a nurse. A press release was handed out to the several hundred members of the press who were able to gain entrance into the suite. It read:

> Due to the incessant pressures on my personal life, legal involvements, and a fairly constant case of cyclothymia, I have decided to enter a peaceful period of self-preservation through the miracle of cryogenics.
>
> This temporary leave of absence will in no way affect my philosophy, business holdings, acquisitions, or a steadfast desire for permanent privacy. I shall return in the near future, when the stock market is more bullish, and I hope to see you all under happier circumstances.
>
> H.R.H.

World-famed photographer Alfred Eisenstadt had four reporters with him from *Life* magazine and he was shooting photos as fast as he could focus and trip the shutter. Under the intense camera lights, a battery of microphones were thrust towards me and reporters shouted questions over one another in total bedlam.

I maintained a steady stream of unintelligible *non sequiturs* in a hoarse whisper, claiming I had a severe case of laryngitus. It was sheer madness exchanging shouted phrases with the news heavyweights:

"Mr. Hughes, I have Richard Hanna, your press representative, on the long-distance phone from Los Angeles. He claims you're not here—"

"That's exactly what I pay him to say. He's doing a good job. Next question."

"How can you prove you really are Howard Hughes?"

"I wouldn't be here if I weren't."

"Come on, sir, admit it. This is some sort of stunt—"

"In the Presidential Suite? At these horrendous rates? What kind of stunt would *that* be?"

This interplay went on for another ten minutes and it was time to leave. My aides formed a flying wedge, with the two beefy Pinkerton guards running interference, and I was wheeled at top speed to a private elevator.

The reporters ran down stairs or commandeered waiting elevators to meet me in the lobby. The situation there was unbelievable. A sea of humanity engulfed us as questions were shouted from all sides:

"Where are you going now, Mr. Hughes?"

"Look this way please, sir."

"Can we go with you?"

"Anybody here willing to sell their notes from upstairs? I came late . . . I'll pay five hundred dollars for anything on paper . . . cash!"

Shefter and Rothschild were steering the wheelchair while the other guards formed a circle around us to prevent anyone from tearing my bandages off. I was whisked into the revolving door and there was a loud crunch; we all got stuck! Overanxious reporters had jammed in three to a slot so that nothing budged. Through my narrow eye-slits I noticed syndicated columnist Ann Landers trapped opposite me. She stared and made notes.

Harried hotel employees tried to disengage the door without success. Finally, an engineer arrived and it took him only a minute to unhinge the door. Outside, a huge crowd had formed on the sidewalk blocking any entrance to our waiting limousine.

My aides lifted me high and literally threw me into the back seat of the limousine. Then we took off, tires screeching, followed by a trail of reporters in cars, vans, and taxis.

New York traffic being congested, we eluded most of the pursuers and reached the Sixtieth Street Heliport. Our reserved helicopter lifted off for a ten minute ride to Newark airport with a very curious pilot glancing backward as I removed the bandages.

News reports were already flooding the airwaves and this commentary by CBS news summed up the general media attitude:

The word came last night in telex messages from California. Howard Hughes, the wire said, would hold a press conference in the Presidential Suite of New York's St. Regis Hotel. A skeptical group of reporters and photographers were met at the elevators by a bearded security man with a walkie-talkie. He claimed to work for International Intelligence. At the fifteenth-floor suite two more plainclothes security types with silver-star lapel pins and two uniformed Pinkerton guards checked press credentials. After fifteen minutes or so waiting in the parlor, a set of double doors was opened and behind them was a desk and behind that a wheelchair holding a man with his head wrapped in a surgical bandage. On his hands were white gloves. The man claimed to be Howard Hughes but refused to offer a handwriting sample, fingerprints, or to speak on the telephone with Frank McCollough of *Time* magazine who knows the real Hughes. . . . We did contact Hughes's spokesman Richard Hannah after the twenty minute encounter at the St. Regis and he again emphatically denied that the man in question was the real Hughes. He theorized that the hoax may have been engineered by Hughes's enemies to force the billionaire into the open where he could be served with a subpoena. . . . The last we saw of the bogus Mr. Hughes he was being raced through the St. Regis lobby in a wheelchair, getting jammed in the revolving door and actually thrown into the waiting limousine. . . . There's little doubt that the whole thing was a bizzare put-on but by whom and why?

The next day a very disturbed Howard Hughes in Vancouver issued this statement to the press: "The imposter who posed as me in New York undoubtedly represents a dissident faction attempting to gain control of my empire. Well, it won't work and I want them to know that!"

Newsman Gabe Pressman tracked me down a week later and I was invited to tell my story before a group of pooled reporters on the evening news over WNEW-TV and other Metromedia stations. At the conclusion of this exposé, a reporter from the crowd asked:

"Did you and your friends have a lot of fun with this caper?"

"Well, obviously—"

At that moment, somebody from my blind side threw a pie that caught me square in the face. It was an appropriate gesture and I had to join in the laughter.

I never did get my script back.

I, Alan Abel, author of *How to Thrive on Rejection: A Manual for Survival*, hereby certify that the contents of this book are 99% accurate.*

_____ L.S.

State of New York
County of New York

Sworn to before me

15 day of May 84

EDWARD S. MALKASSIAN
Notary Public, State of New York
No. 31-7679800
Qualified in New York County
Commission Expires March 30, 1986

*Some names have been changed to protect the guilty.